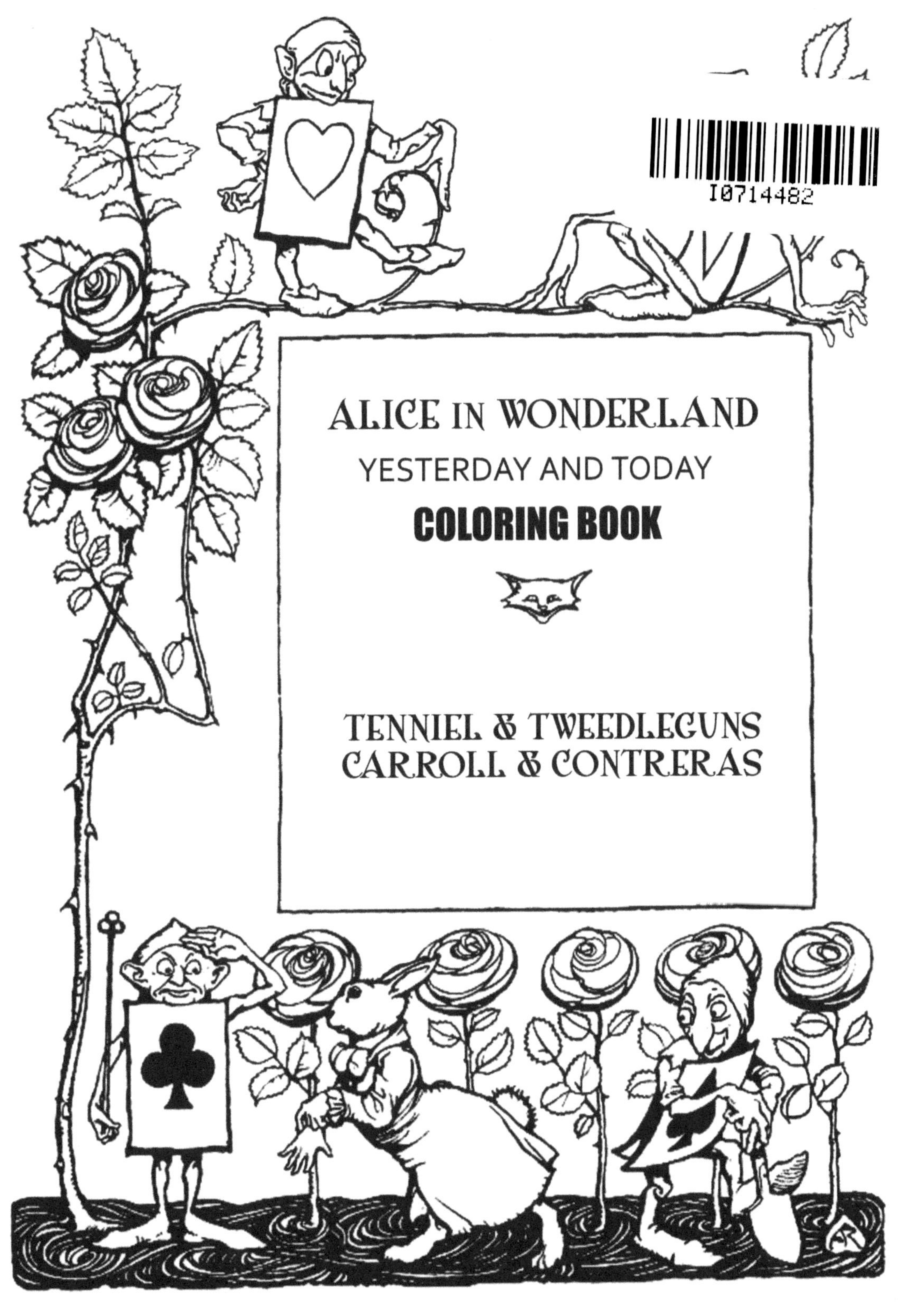

ALICE IN WONDERLAND

YESTERDAY AND TODAY

COLORING BOOK

TENNIEL & TWEEDLEGUNS
CARROLL & CONTRERAS

ISBN 978-1-936517-94-7
For Bulk Sales or Permissions contact the Publisher at:
Other Realms Press
A Division of Micro Publishing Media, INC
www.MPMstore.com
PO Box 1522
Stockbrdige, MA 01262

For more information about Raúl Alberto Contreras
www.dementedentertainment.com

Original quotes and illustrations by Lewis Carroll and Sir John Tenniel
Additional Embellishments by Raúl Alberto Contreras and Tweedle Guns

INTRODUCTION

One hundred and Fifty years ago one of the most influential books of all time was published, Lewis Carroll's "Alice's Adventures in Wonderland." The artwork was done by Sir John Tenniel, the premiere illustrator in the United Kingdom at the time. His Wonderland artwork, done at the end of his career, became the pinnacle of his work. You have some of those amazing illustrations in front of you.

A mere 3 years ago, Raúl Alberto Contreras printed his own modern and twisted book called, "Alice's Bloody Adventures in Wonderland." He enlisted the help of Los Angeles street artist, "Tweedle Guns" to illustrate his book. Raúl's idea was to mutate the original John Tenniel's into his new vison.

Raul's thought was that..."maybe one day, The Doctor (Who) would find the book flip through it thinking it was the original, then stopping, and saying 'Wait a minute, this isn't right!" Then getting into the Tardis to see what went wrong."

This book starts in the past and brings you to the present. You will be able to compare and contrast Tenniel's and Tweedle Guns' work, as you color them in any way you like!

Happy coloring!

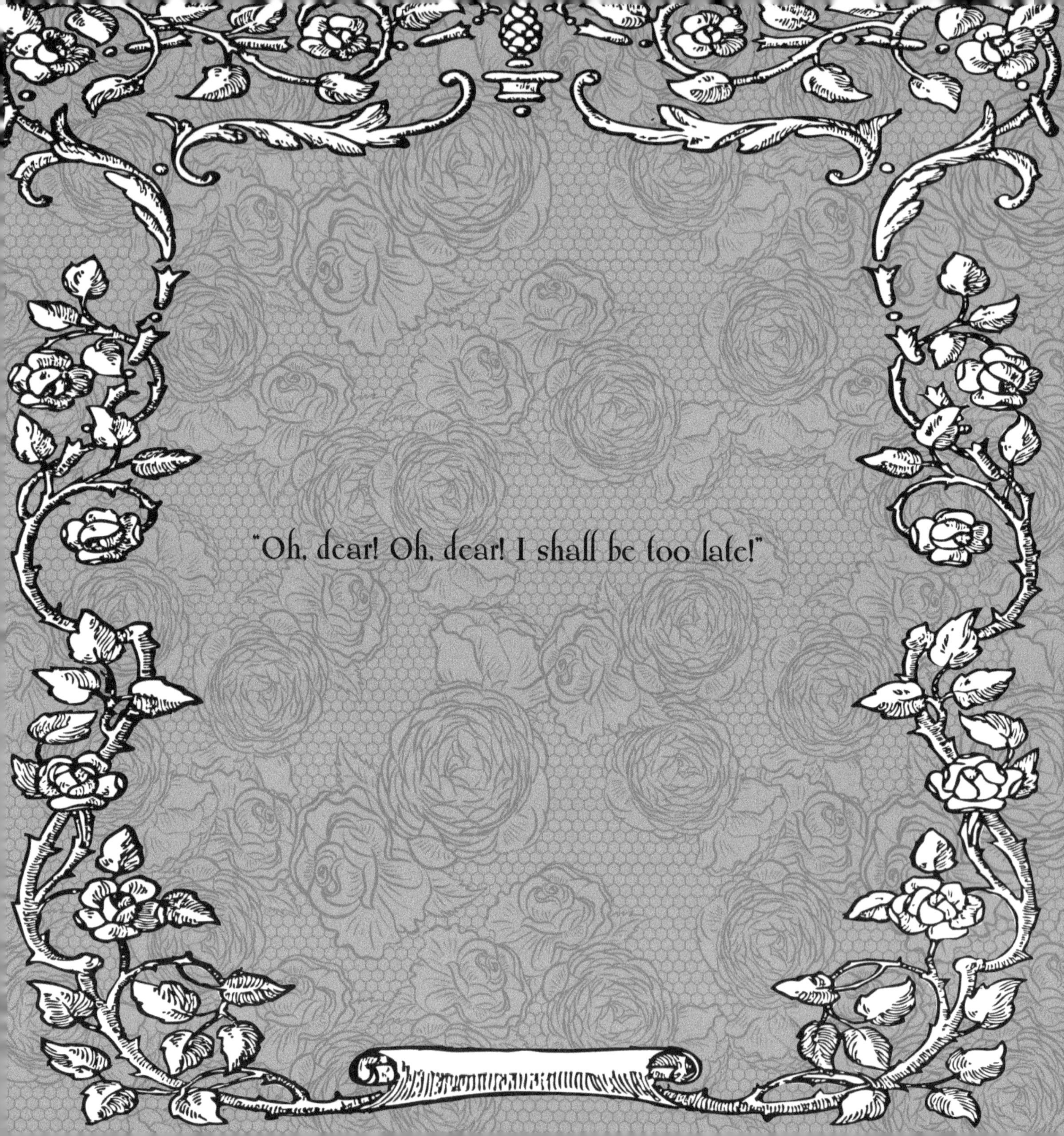

"Oh, dear! Oh, dear! I shall be too late!"

"Oh, the Duchess, the Duchess! Oh won't she be savage if I've kept her waiting!"

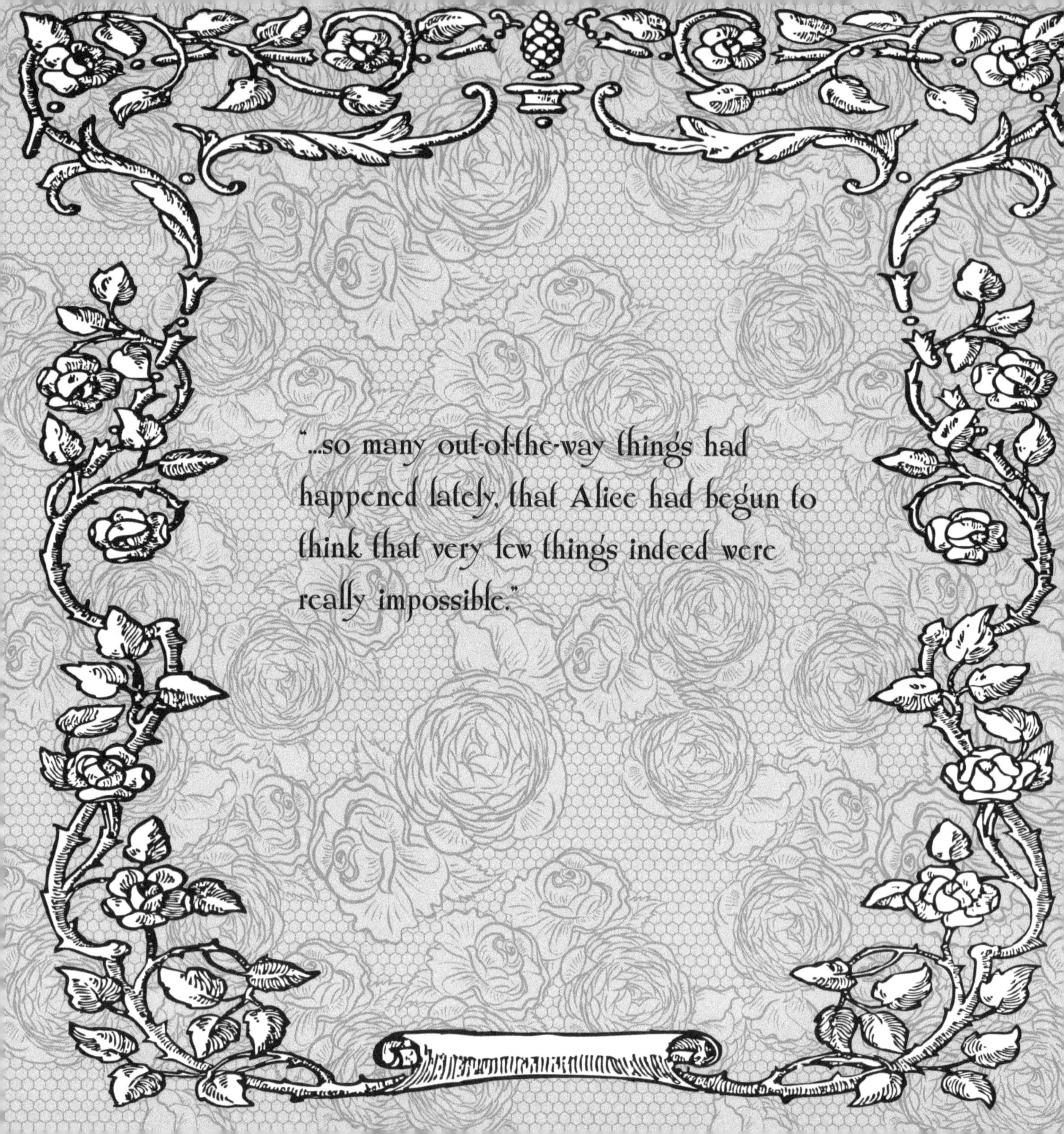

"...so many out-of-the-way things had happened lately, that Alice had begun to think that very few things indeed were really impossible."

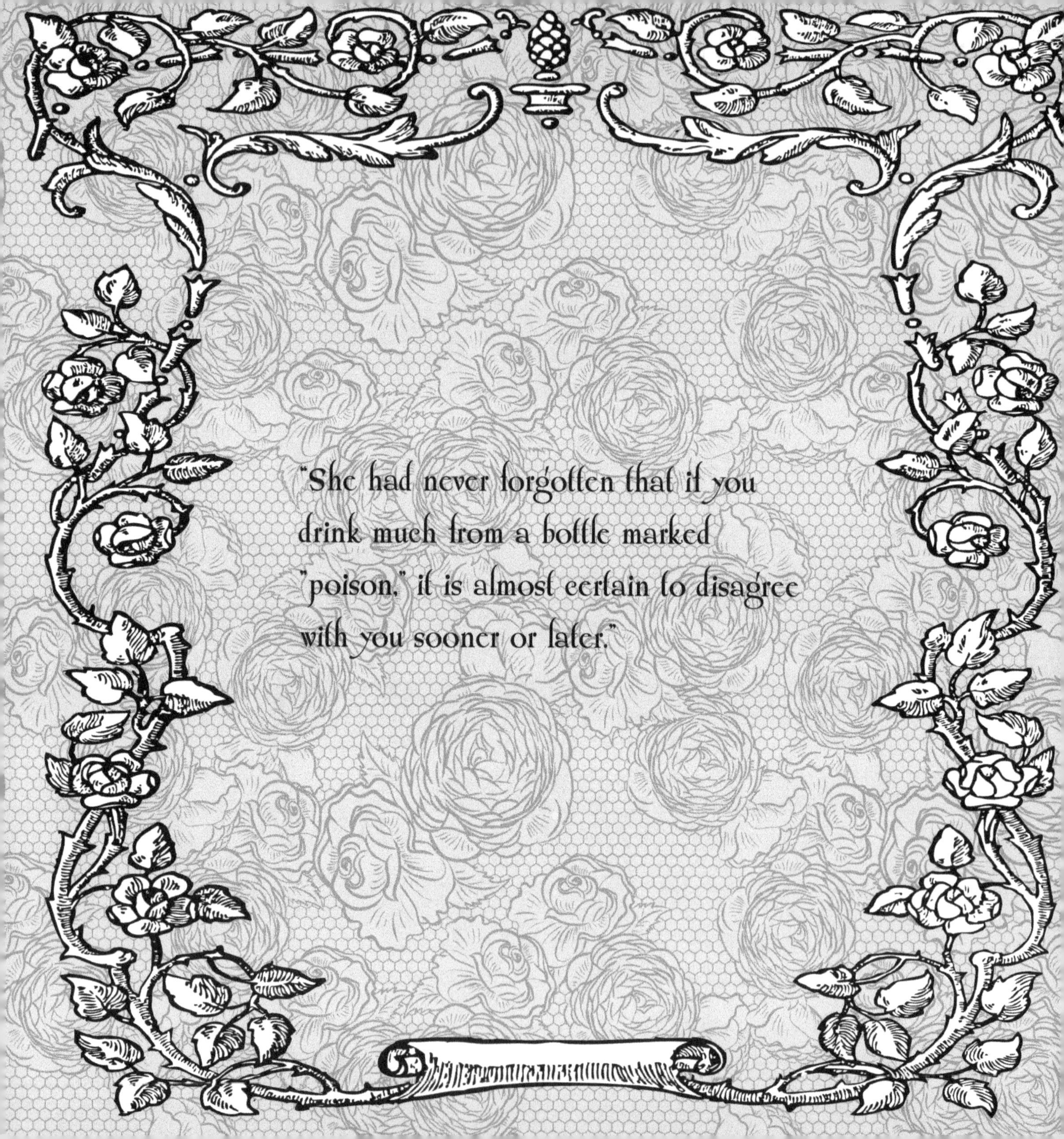

"She had never forgotten that if you drink much from a bottle marked "poison," it is almost certain to disagree with you sooner or later."

DRINK

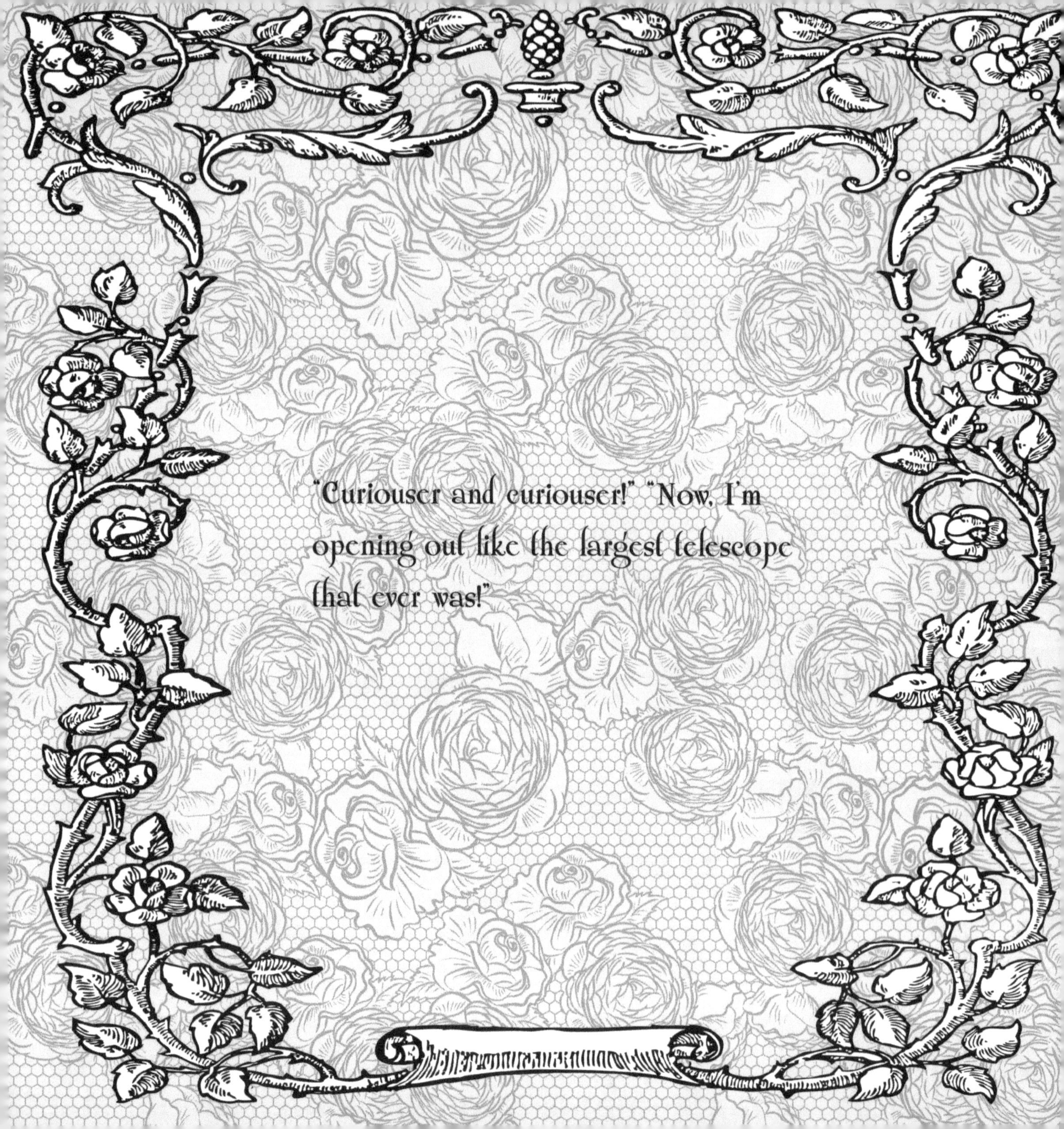

"Curiouser and curiouser!" "Now, I'm opening out like the largest telescope that ever was!"

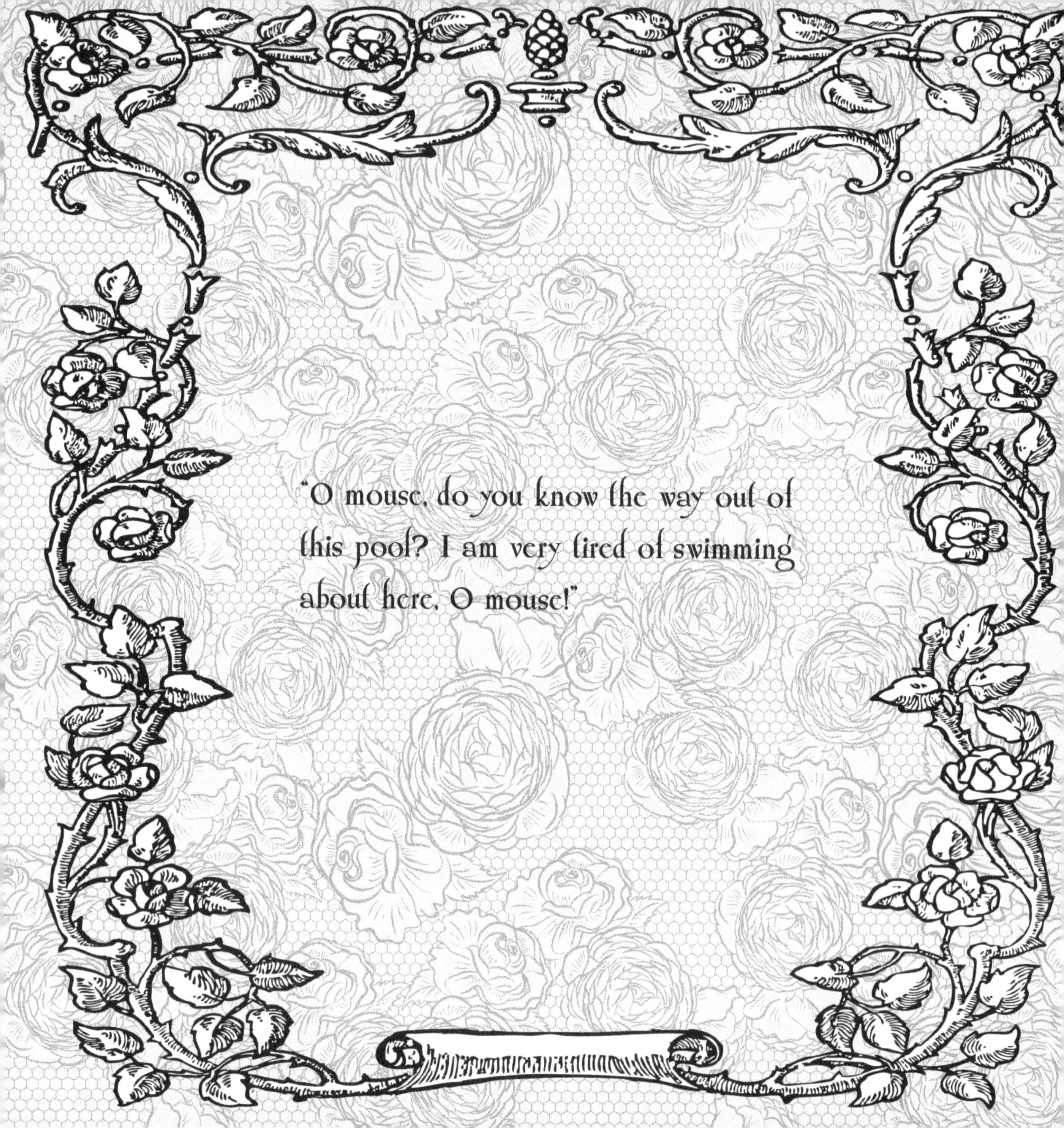

"O mouse, do you know the way out of this pool? I am very tired of swimming about here, O mouse!"

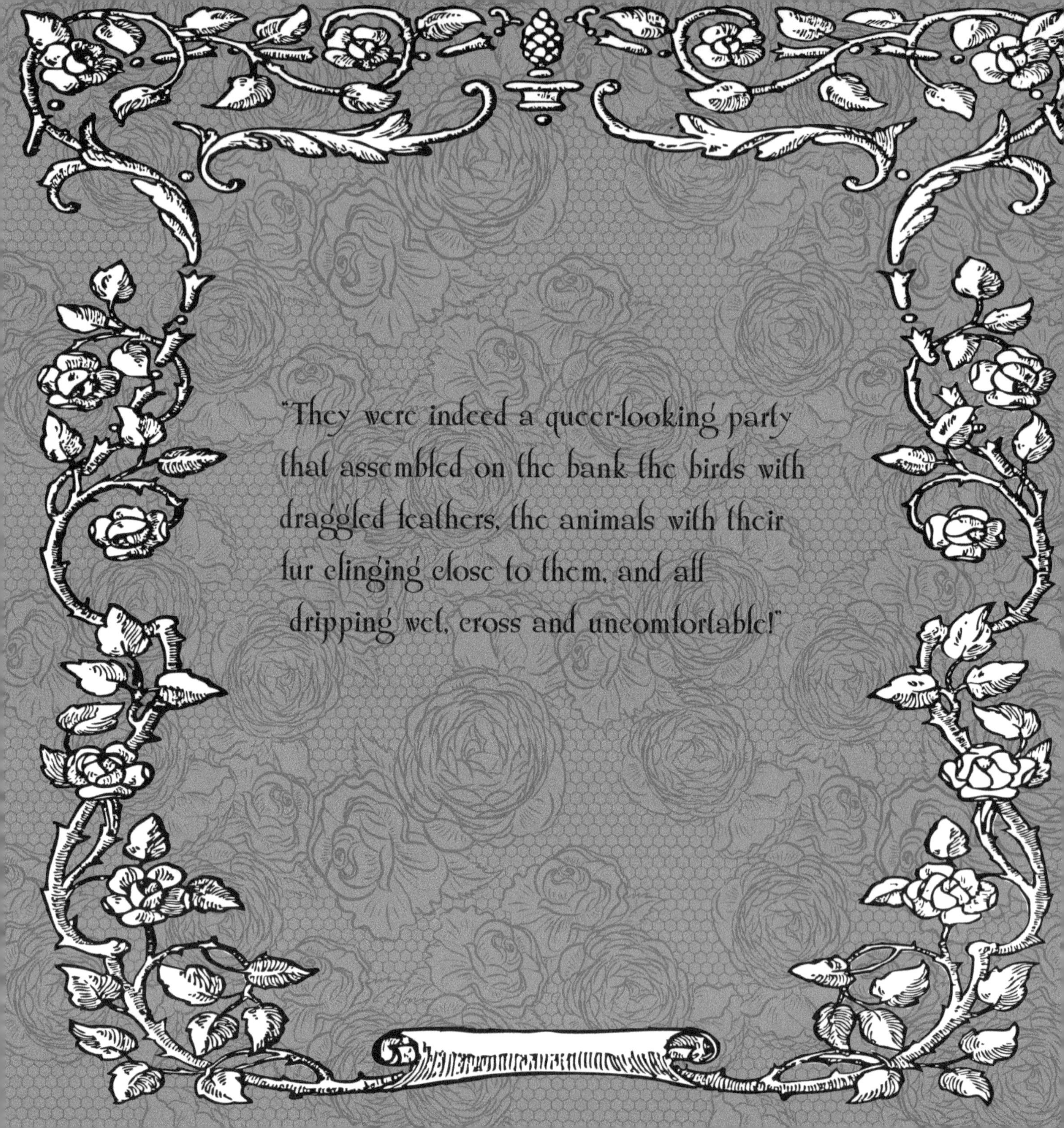

"They were indeed a queer-looking party that assembled on the bank the birds with draggled feathers, the animals with their fur clinging close to them, and all dripping wet, cross and uncomfortable!"

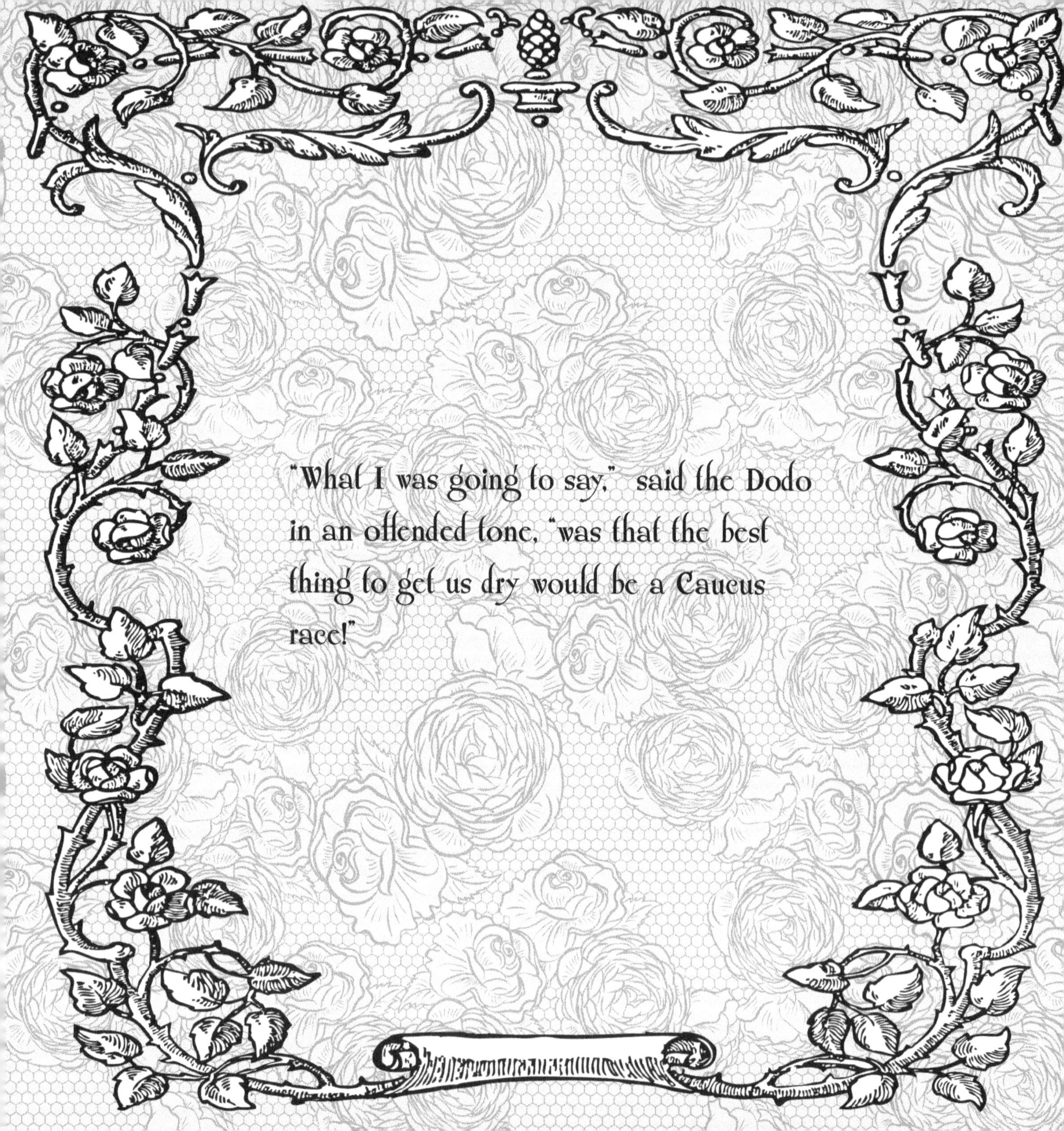

"What I was going to say," said the Dodo in an offended tone, "was that the best thing to get us dry would be a Caucus race!"

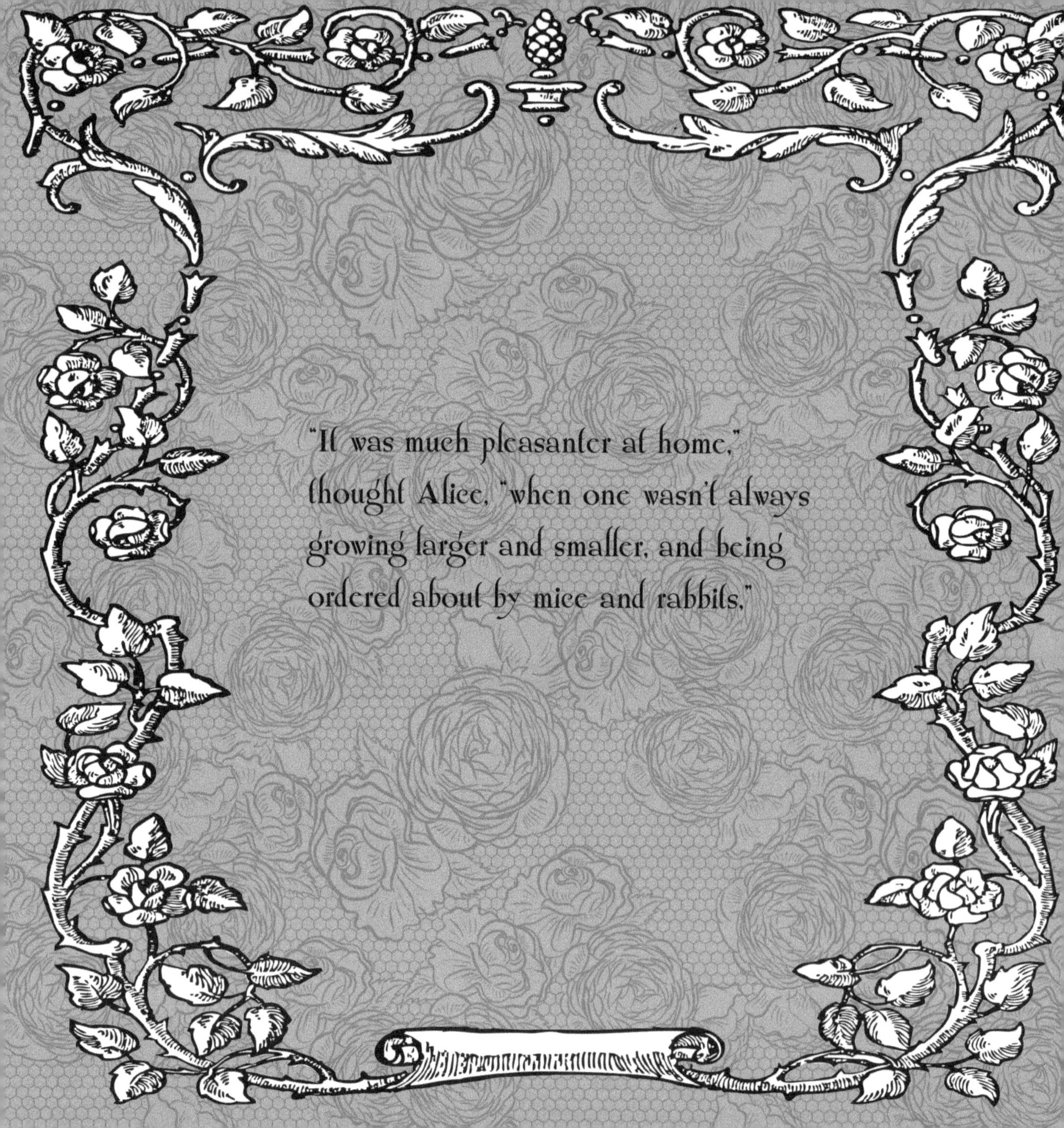

"It was much pleasanter at home," thought Alice, "when one wasn't always growing larger and smaller, and being ordered about by mice and rabbits."

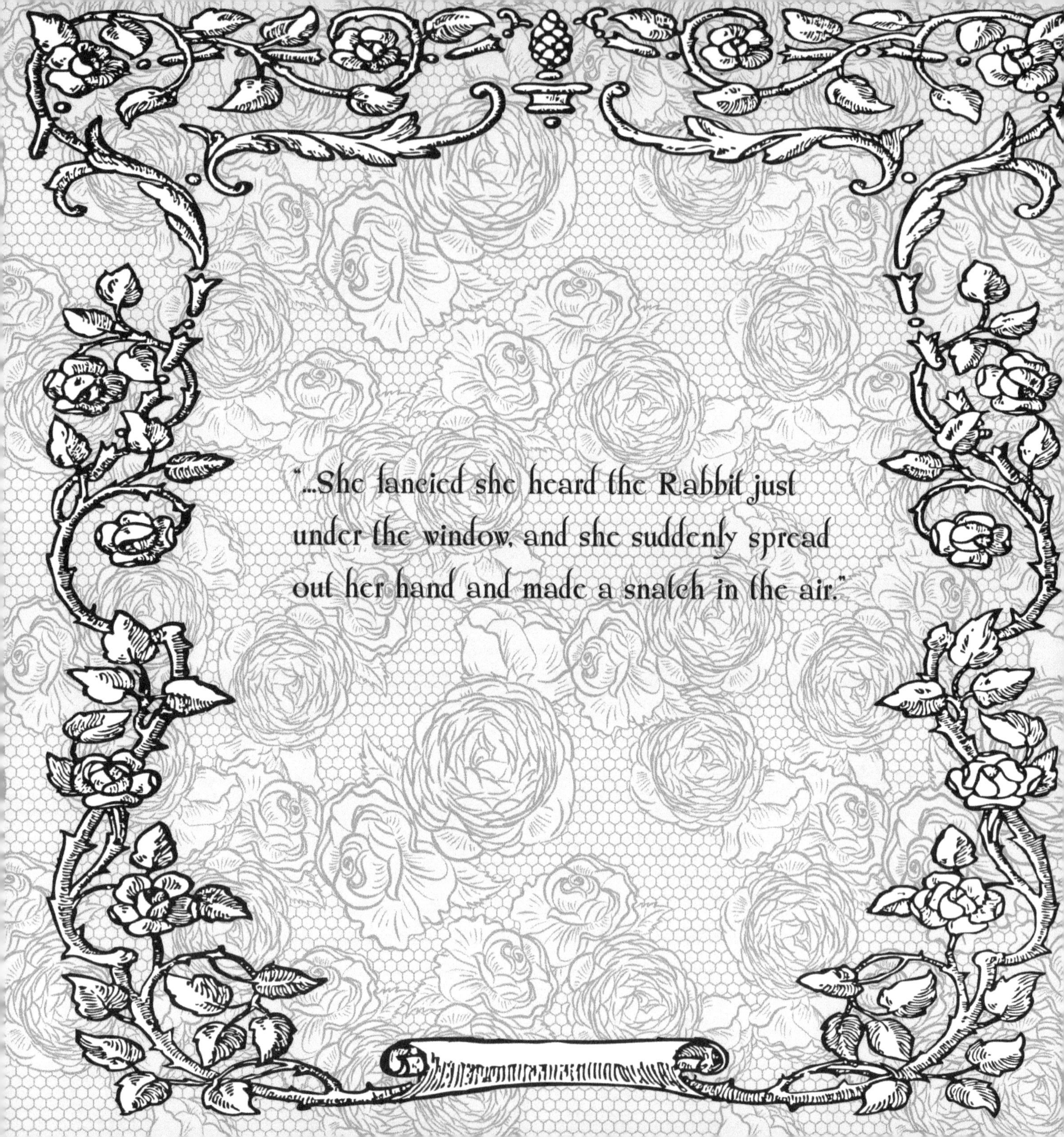

"...She fancied she heard the Rabbit just
under the window, and she suddenly spread
out her hand and made a snatch in the air."

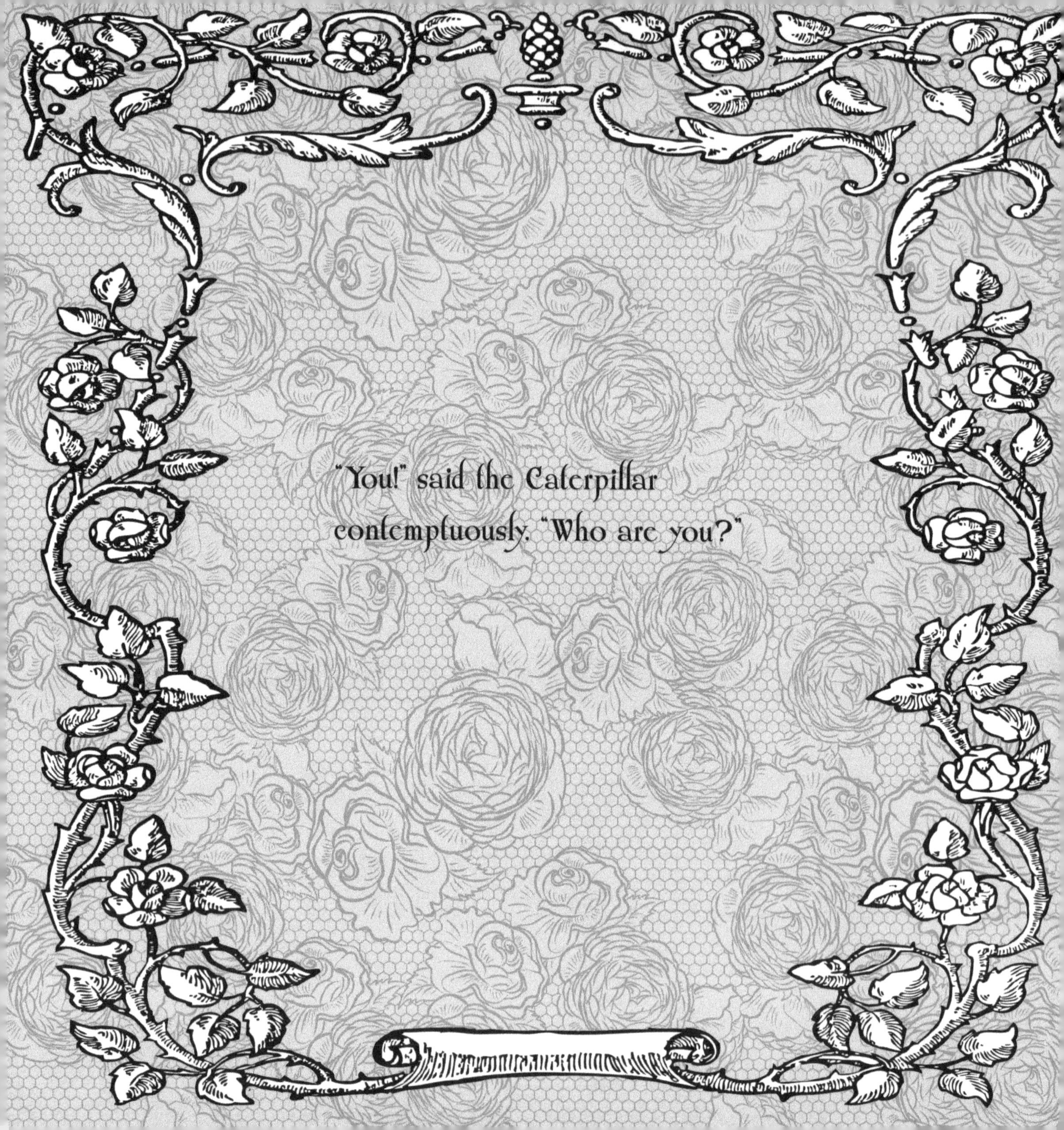

"You!" said the Caterpillar contemptuously. "Who are you?"

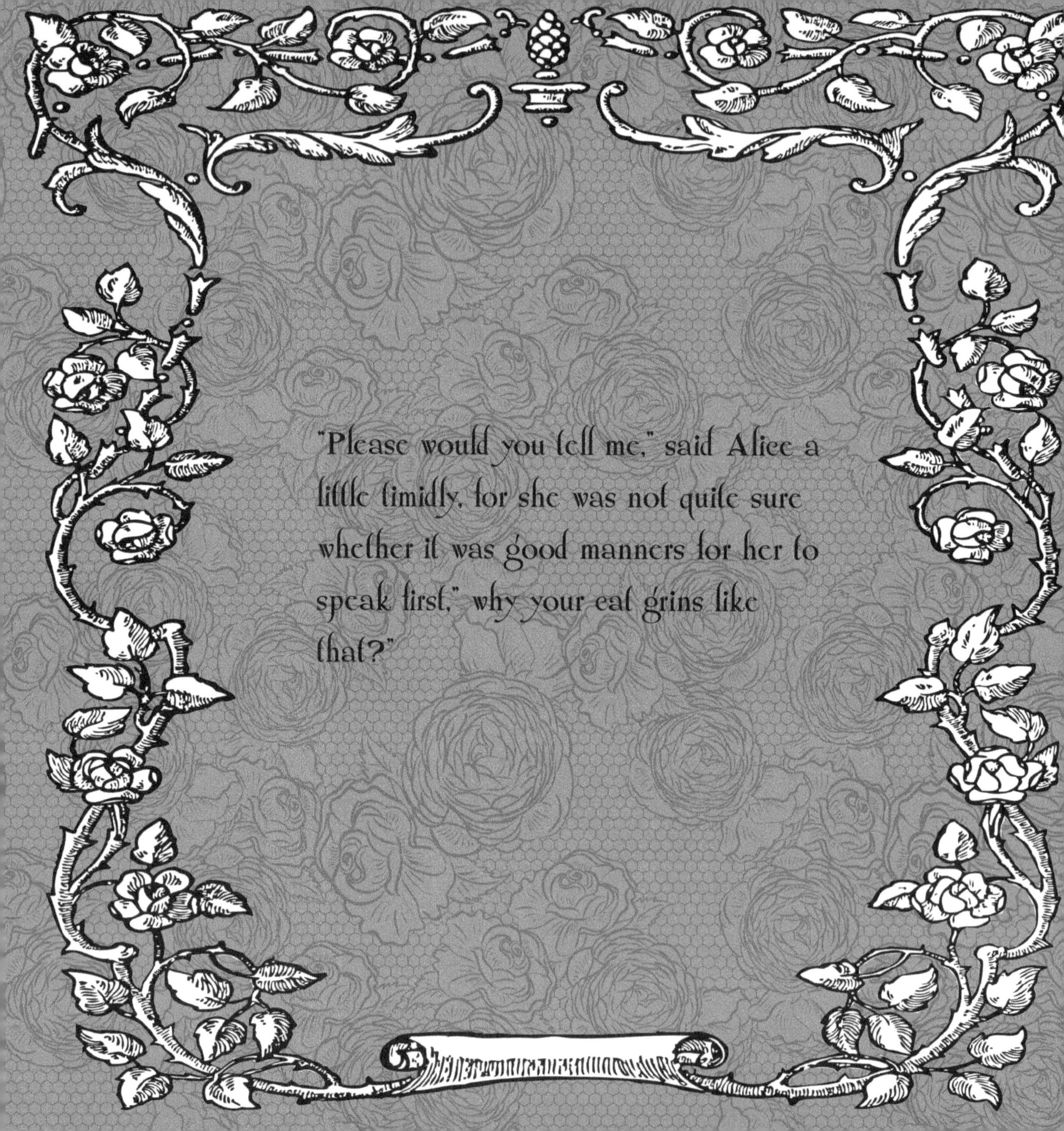

"Please would you tell me," said Alice a little timidly, for she was not quite sure whether it was good manners for her to speak first," why your cat grins like that?"

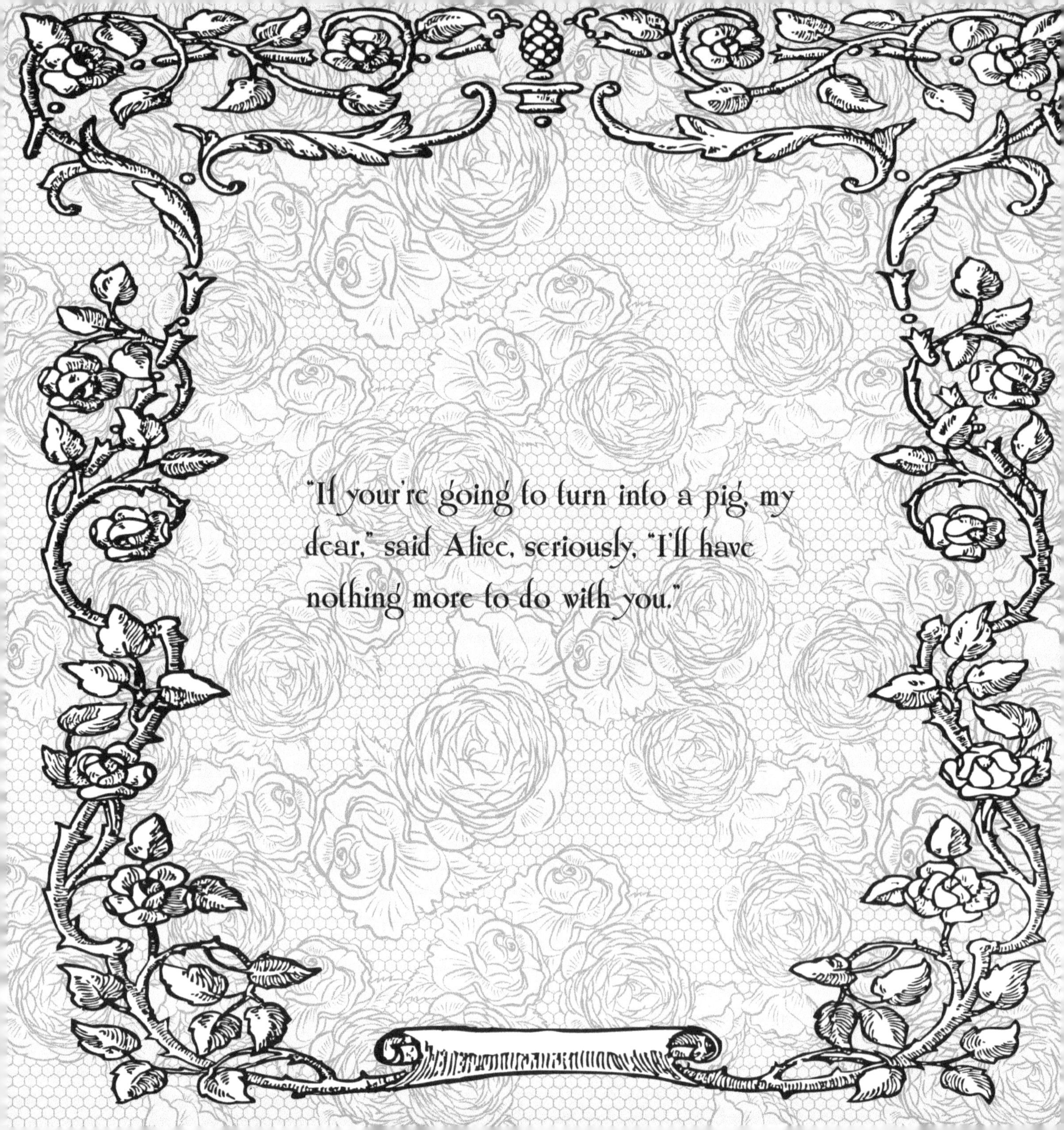

"If your're going to turn into a pig, my dear," said Alice, seriously, "I'll have nothing more to do with you."

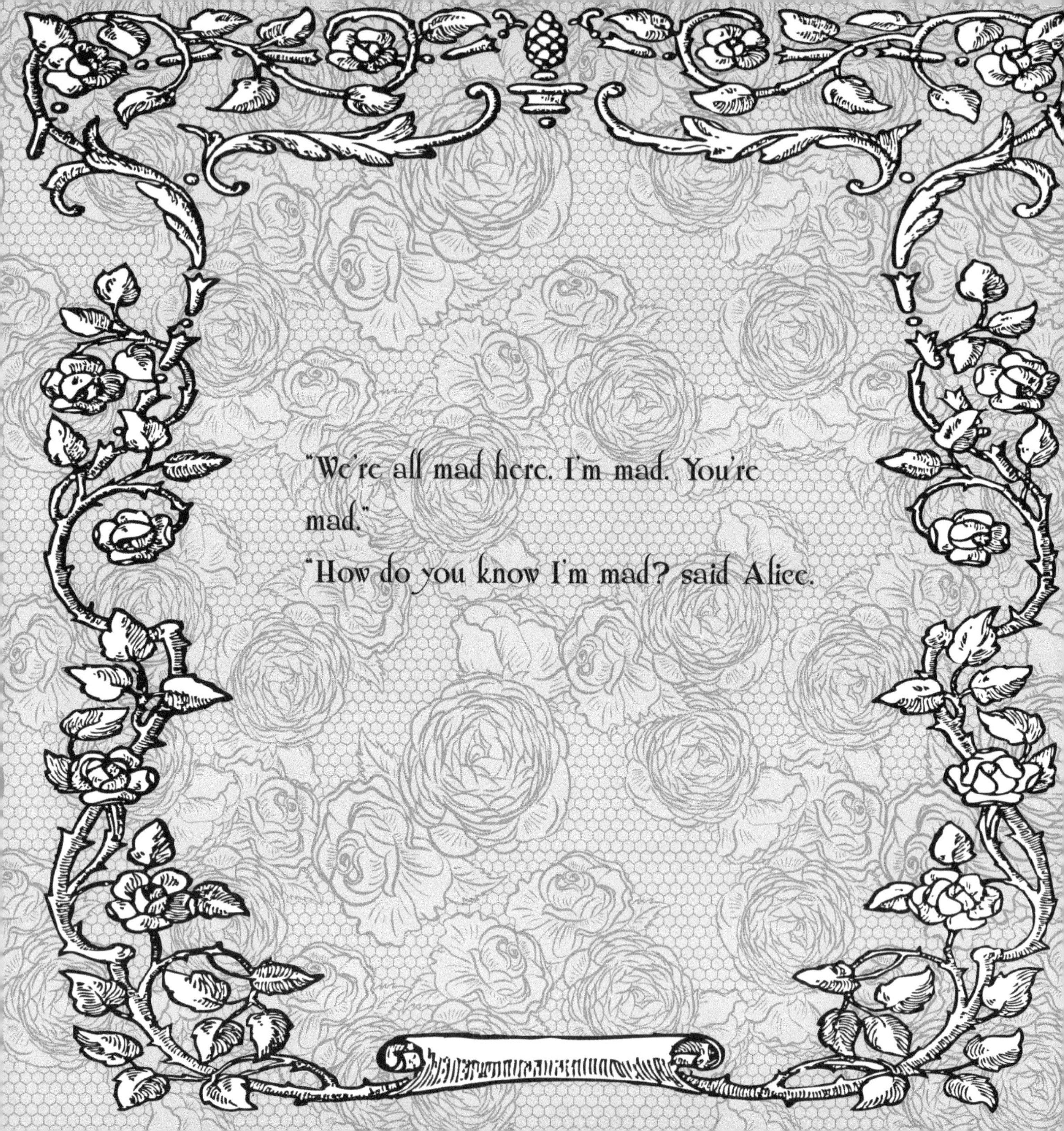

"We're all mad here. I'm mad. You're mad."

"How do you know I'm mad? said Alice.

"Twinkle, twinkle, little bat!
How I wonder what you're at!"
"You know that song, perhaps?"
"I've heard something like it,"
said Alice.
"It goes on, you know," the Hatter
continued, "in this way."
"Up above the world you fly,
Like a tea-tray in the sky.
Twinkle, twinkle."

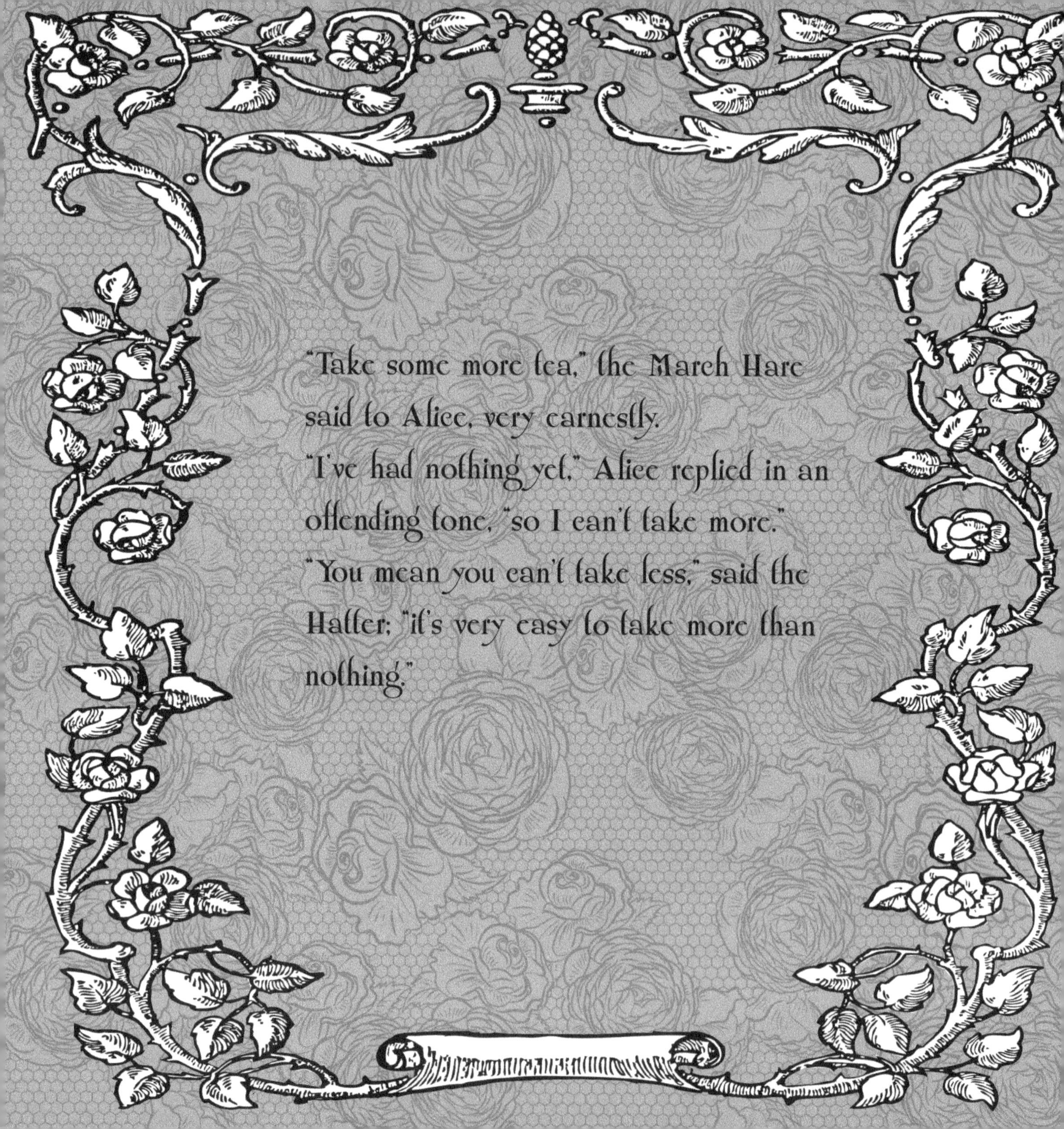

"Take some more tea," the March Hare said to Alice, very earnestly.

"I've had nothing yet," Alice replied in an offending tone, "so I can't take more."

"You mean you can't take less," said the Hatter; "it's very easy to take more than nothing."

In this Style
10/6

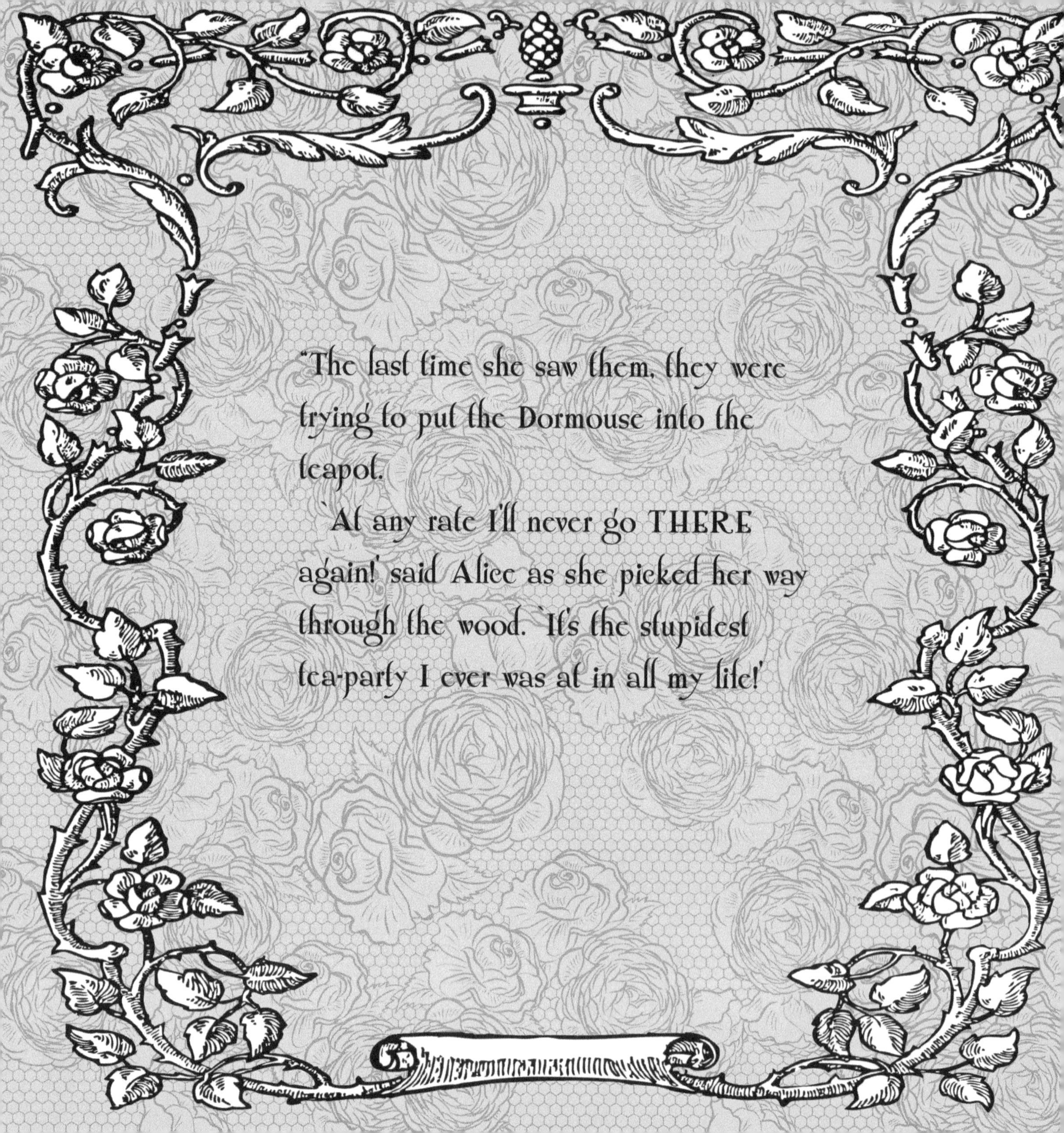

"The last time she saw them, they were trying to put the Dormouse into the teapot.

`At any rate I'll never go THERE again!' said Alice as she picked her way through the wood. `It's the stupidest tea-party I ever was at in all my life!'

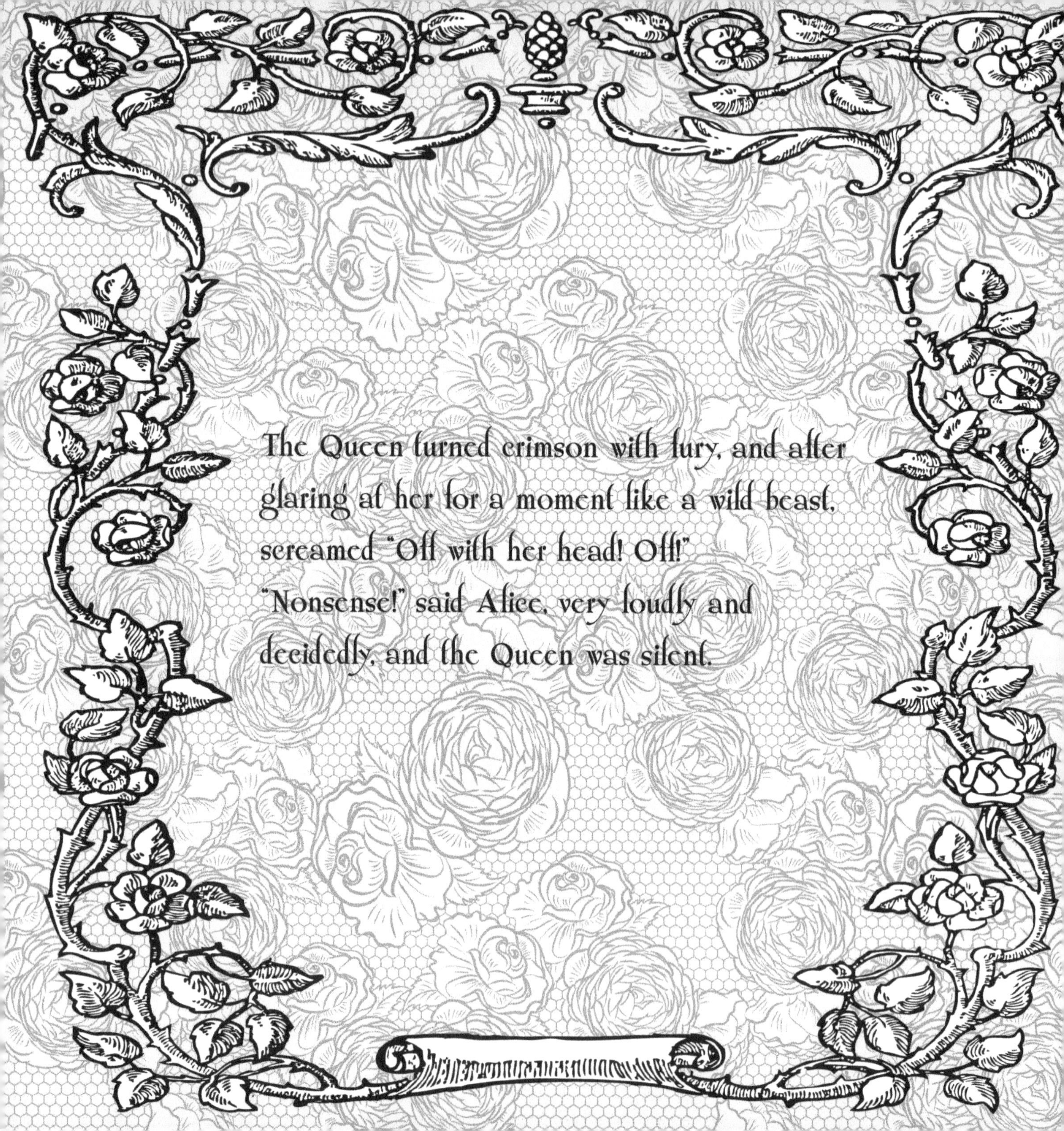

The Queen turned crimson with fury, and after glaring at her for a moment like a wild beast, screamed "Off with her head! Off!"

"Nonsense!" said Alice, very loudly and decidedly, and the Queen was silent.

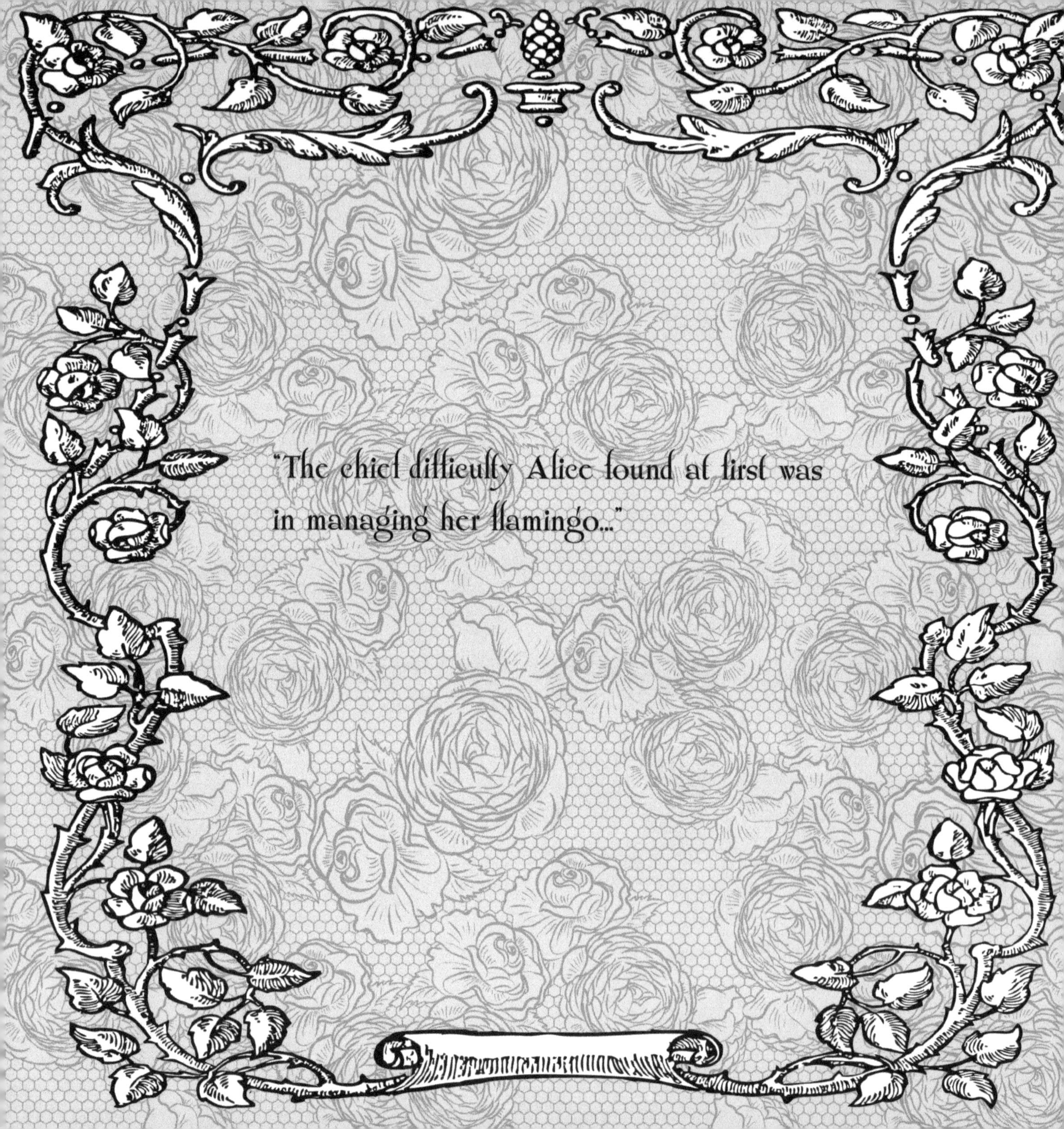

"The chief difficulty Alice found at first was in managing her flamingo..."

The King's argument was, that anything that had a head could be beheaded, and that you weren't to talk nonsense.

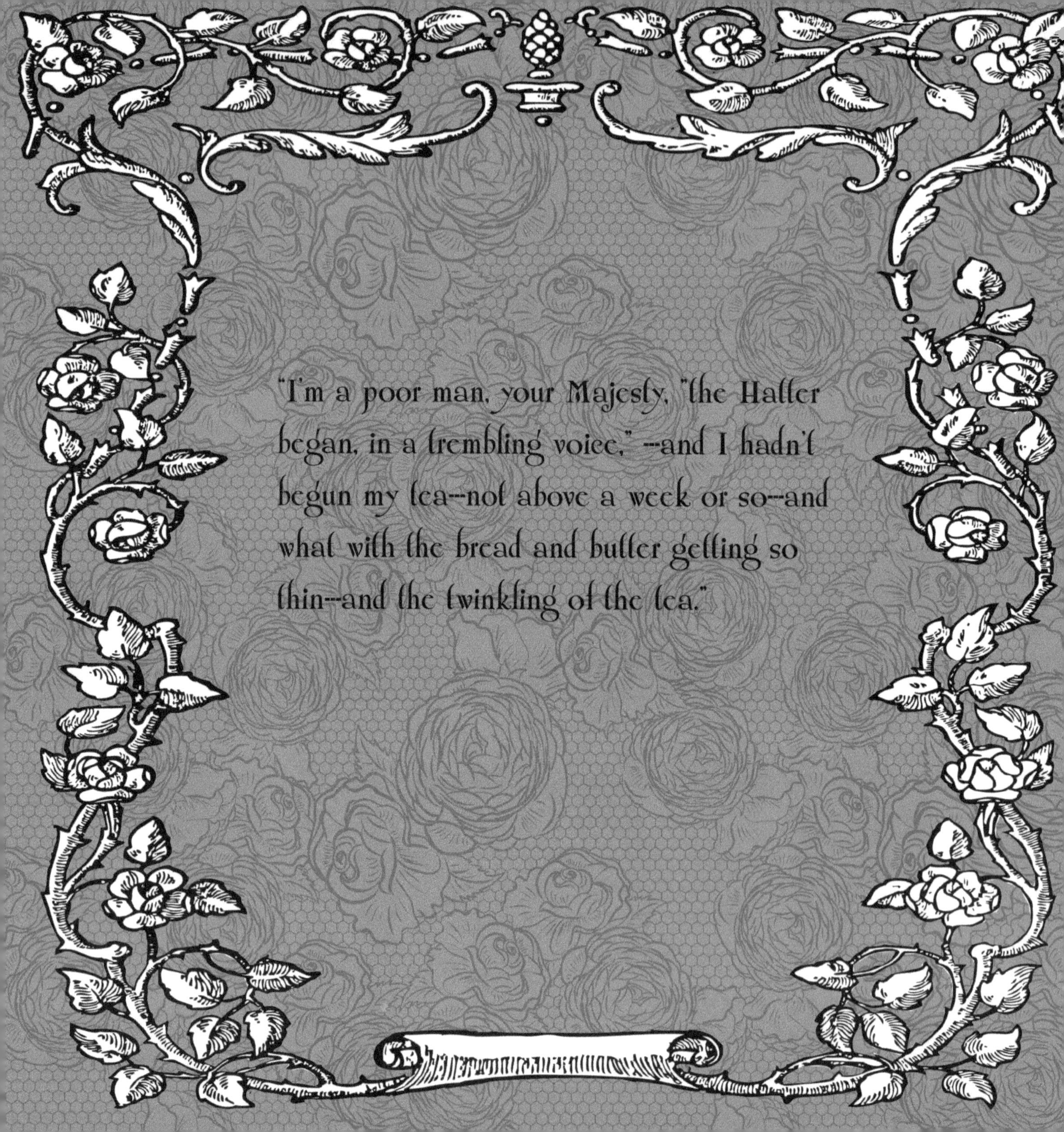

"I'm a poor man, your Majesty, "the Hatter began, in a trembling voice," --and I hadn't begun my tea--not above a week or so--and what with the bread and butter getting so thin--and the twinkling of the tea."

In this Style 10/6

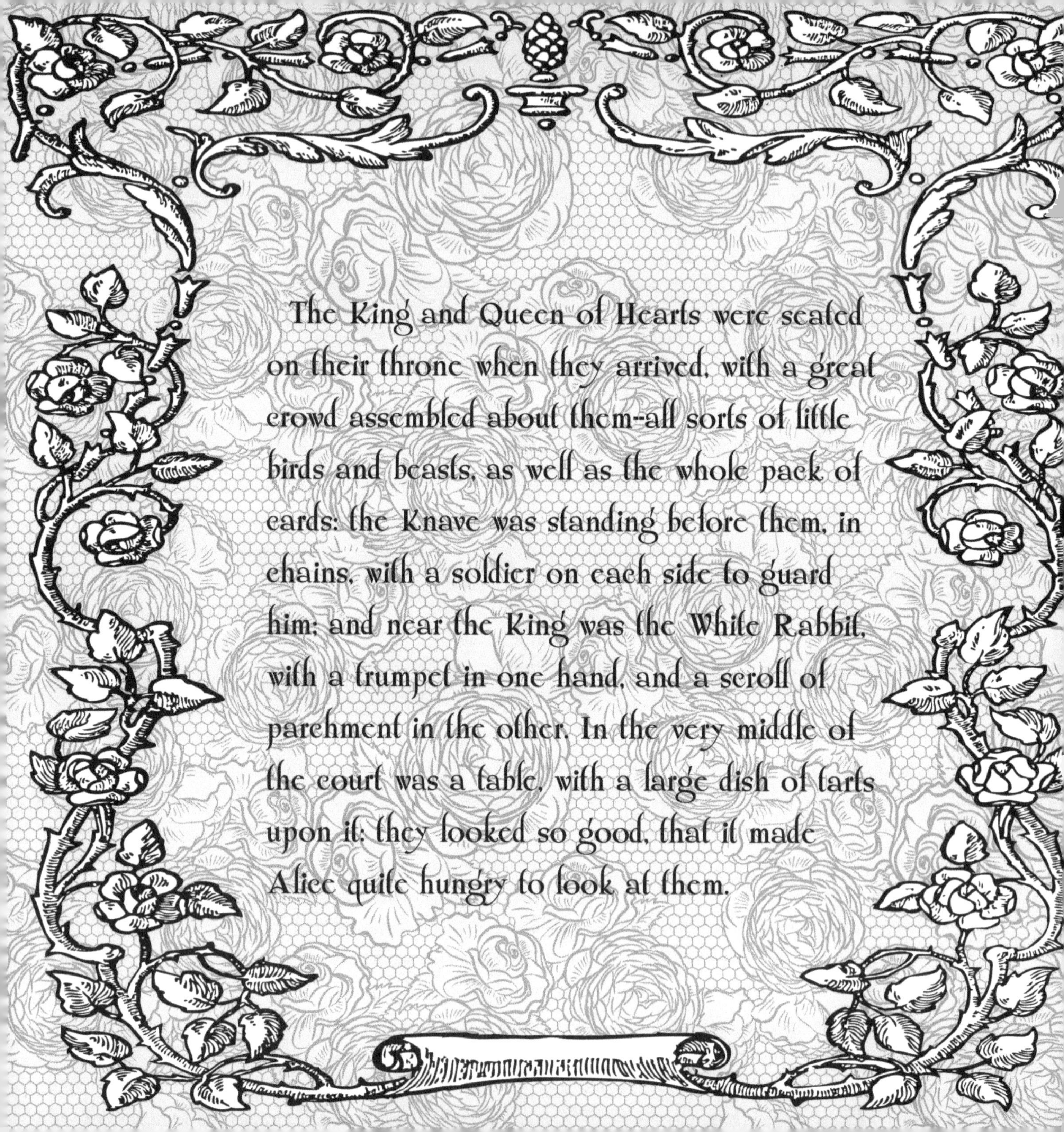

The King and Queen of Hearts were seated on their throne when they arrived, with a great crowd assembled about them--all sorts of little birds and beasts, as well as the whole pack of cards: the Knave was standing before them, in chains, with a soldier on each side to guard him; and near the King was the White Rabbit, with a trumpet in one hand, and a scroll of parchment in the other. In the very middle of the court was a table, with a large dish of tarts upon it: they looked so good, that it made Alice quite hungry to look at them.

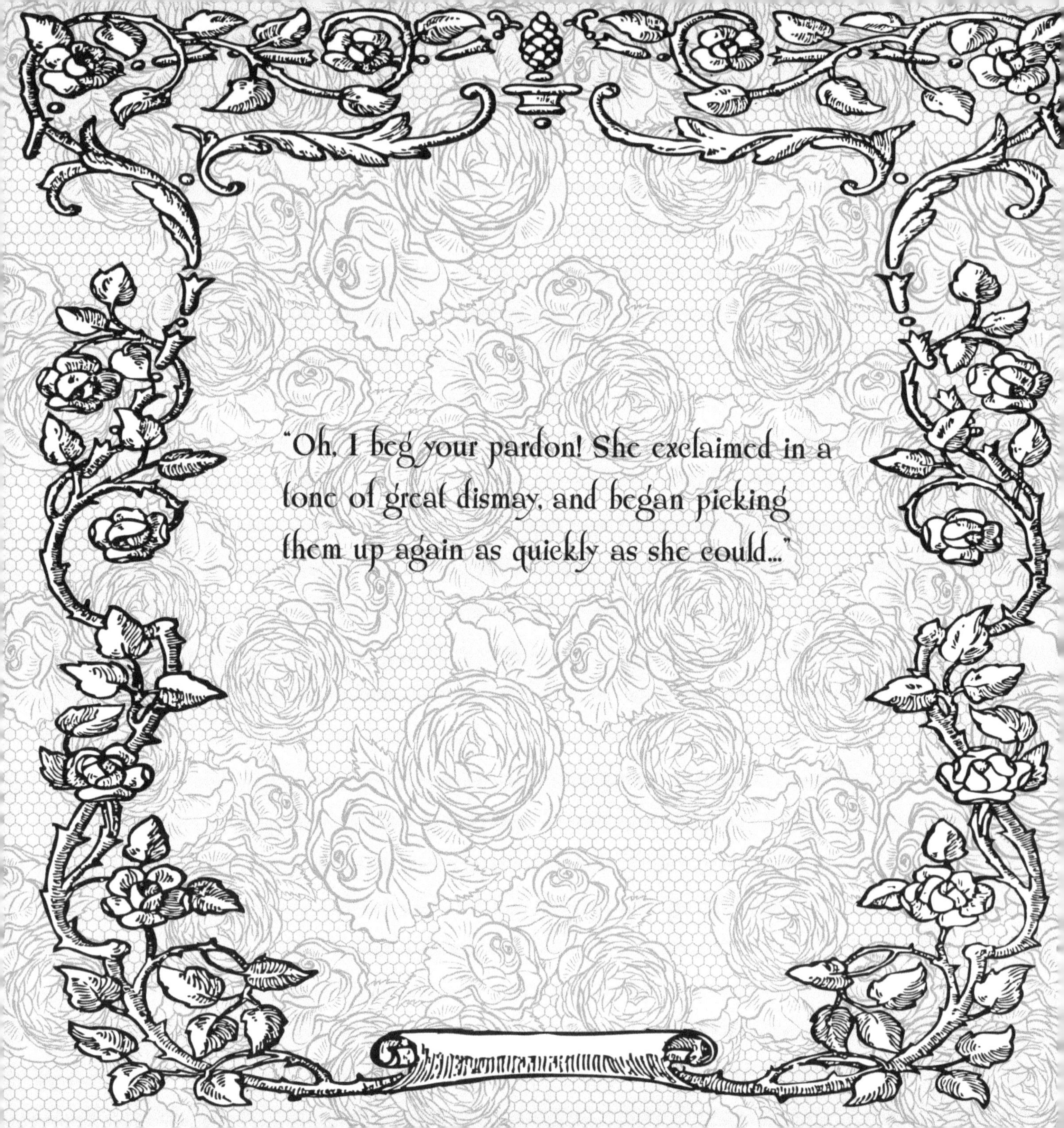

"Oh, I beg your pardon! She exclaimed in a tone of great dismay, and began picking them up again as quickly as she could..."

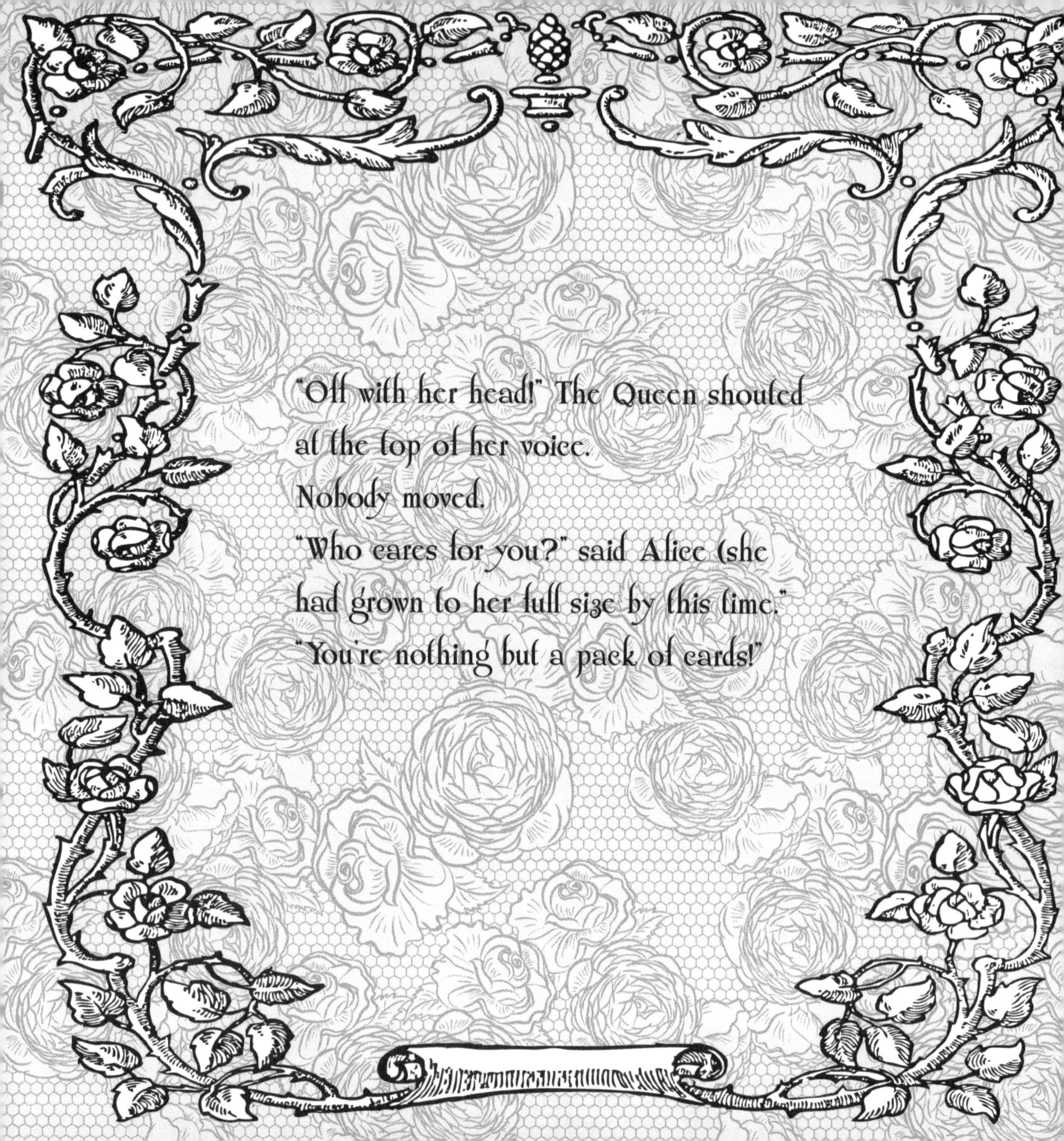

"Off with her head!" The Queen shouted at the top of her voice.
Nobody moved.
"Who cares for you?" said Alice (she had grown to her full size by this time.)
"You're nothing but a pack of cards!"

ALICE Today

Alice was beginning to get very tired of sitting by the river bank and having nothing to do. She lay back upon the grass and looked up at the chemtrails crisscrossing the big blue sky and wondered if the rumors were true that the government was spraying the masses with drugs to make them complacent to the madness of their day-to-day existence.

Her pet cat, Dinah, was amusing herself by chasing purple butterflies across the grass field. Edith, Alice's dark-haired older sister, was reading Frank L. Baum's The Land of Oz.

"I'm bored. Bored, bored, bored!"

Alice sighed as she plucked blades of grass out of the ground.

Edith looked disapprovingly down from her book at Alice and said, "You need a book."

"I need my phone, or laptop. Something with a battery in it!" Alice replied defiantly.

"We are on vacation," said Edith, looking back at her book.

"No electronics!" said Alice and Edith in unison, Alice mockingly.

Alice started to her feet, for it flashed across her mind that a fashionable talking rabbit brandishing a deadly weapon and knowledge of time might be somewhat dangerous and fun. At least it should make the boredom of the day go away. Excited, she turned around to Edith and saw a horrific display; her sister lay dead, her throat slit from ear to ear.

Armed with a knife in each hand and vengeance in her eyes, Alice closed in from behind, turned the corner, and tossed the last two knives at the rabbit.

One knife split the hairs between his ears and smacked into the wall next to him as he turned another corner, and the second nicked his jacket.

Around the neck of the bottle was a paper label with the words DRINK ME beautifully printed on it in large latters.

"Okay...Can this place get more random?" thought Alice. For you see, so many random things had happened laterly that Alice had begun to think that very few things were really impossible. It was all very cool to ssay "Drink me?" but Alice, not being an idiot, was not going to do that in a hurry.

DRINK ME

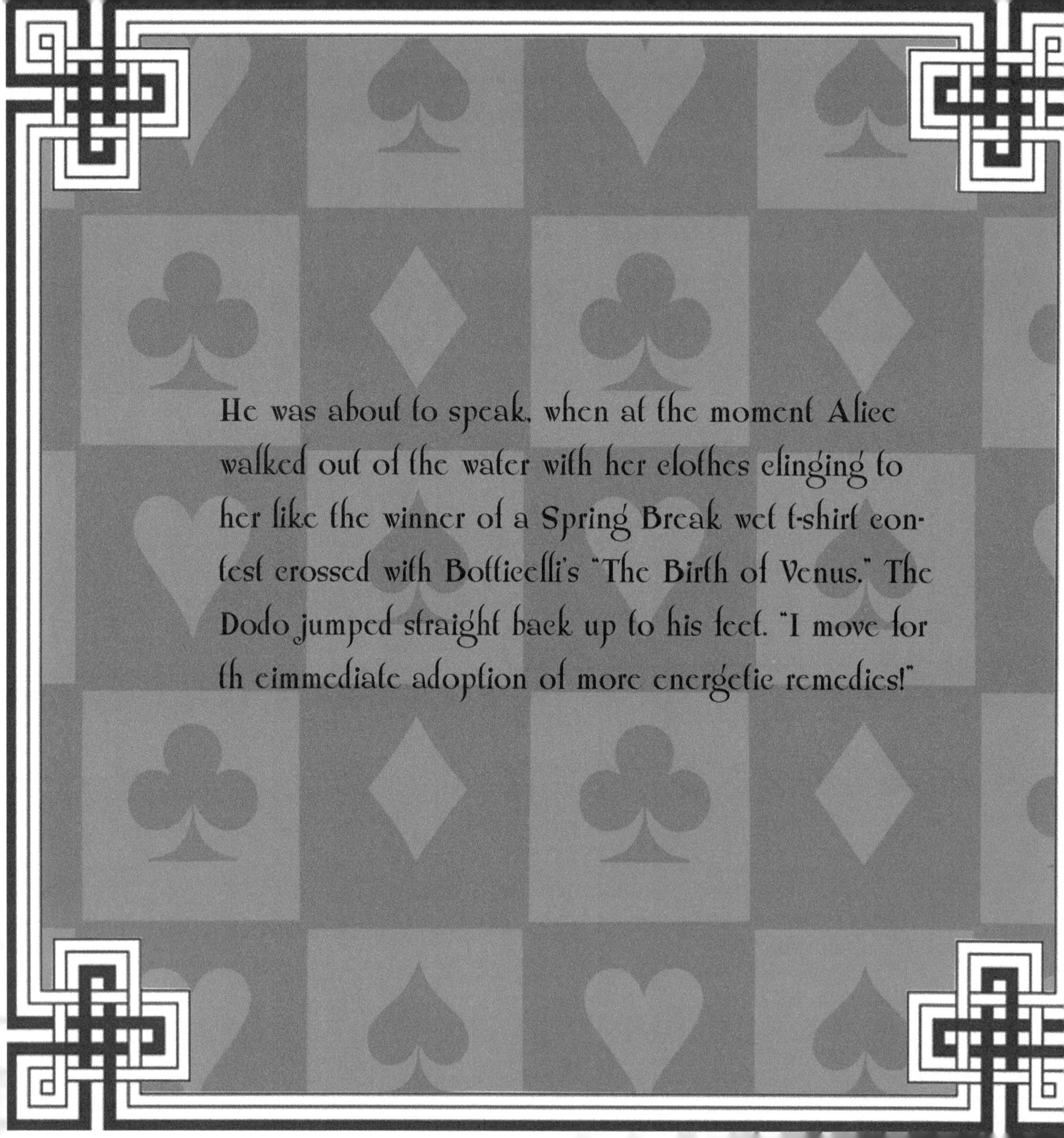

He was about to speak, when at the moment Alice walked out of the water with her clothes clinging to her like the winner of a Spring Break wet t-shirt contest crossed with Botticelli's "The Birth of Venus." The Dodo jumped straight back up to his feet. "I move for th eimmediate adoption of more energetic remedies!"

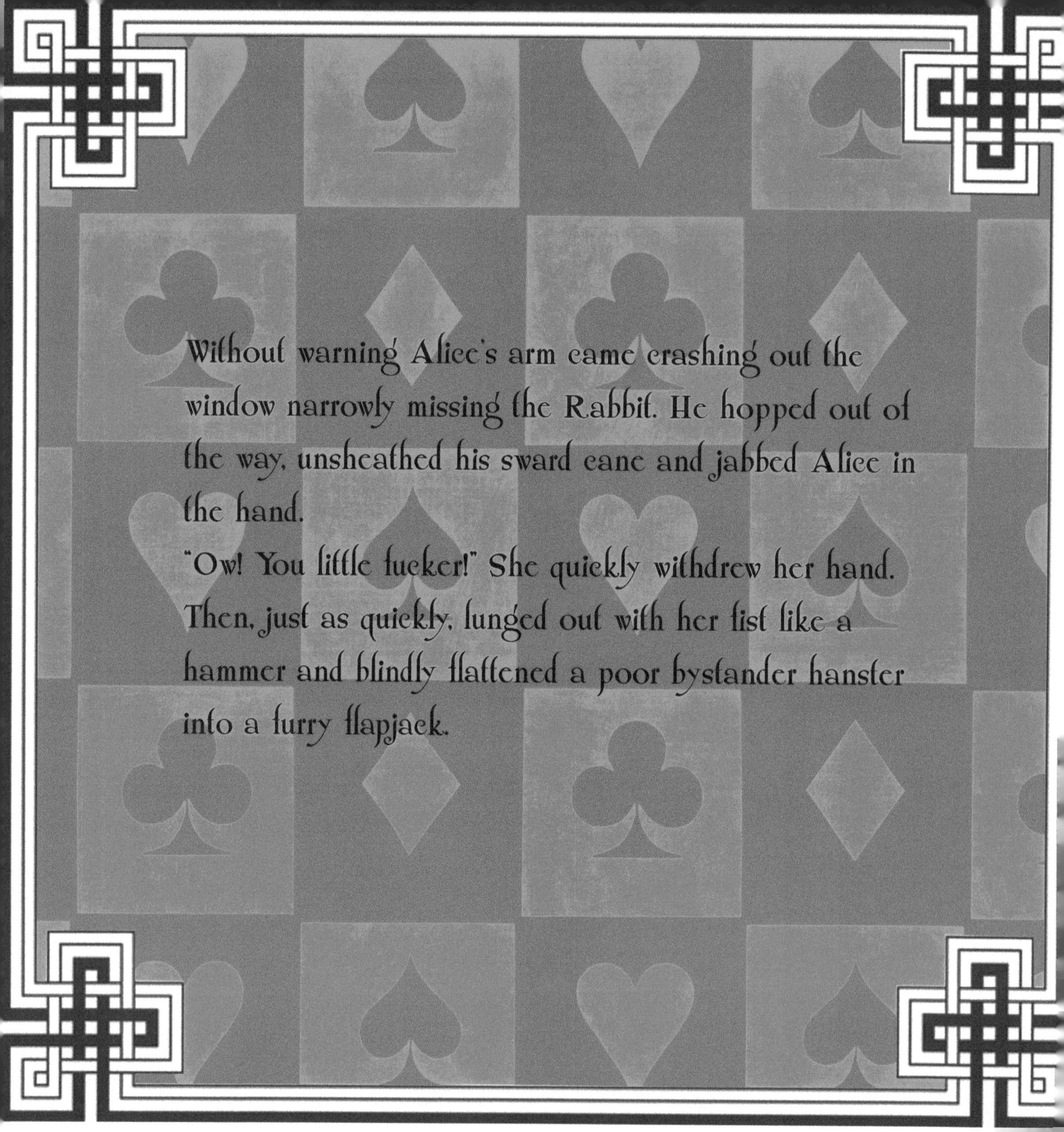

Without warning Alice's arm came crashing out the window narrowly missing the Rabbit. He hopped out of the way, unsheathed his sward cane and jabbed Alice in the hand.

"Ow! You little fucker!" She quickly withdrew her hand. Then, just as quickly, lunged out with her fist like a hammer and blindly flattened a poor bystander hanster into a furry flapjack.

"Who are you? You look like you need to unwind," said the Caterpillar.

This was not an encouraging operning for a coversation, yet Alice nodded in agreement, already transfixed by his hypotic presence, and replied rather shyly, "It has been a crazy day. I am wound up hard and I don't think I am normal anymore."

"Freaking out. Right on. I dig. You can chill here and get groovy within the universe with me, " said the Caterpillar.

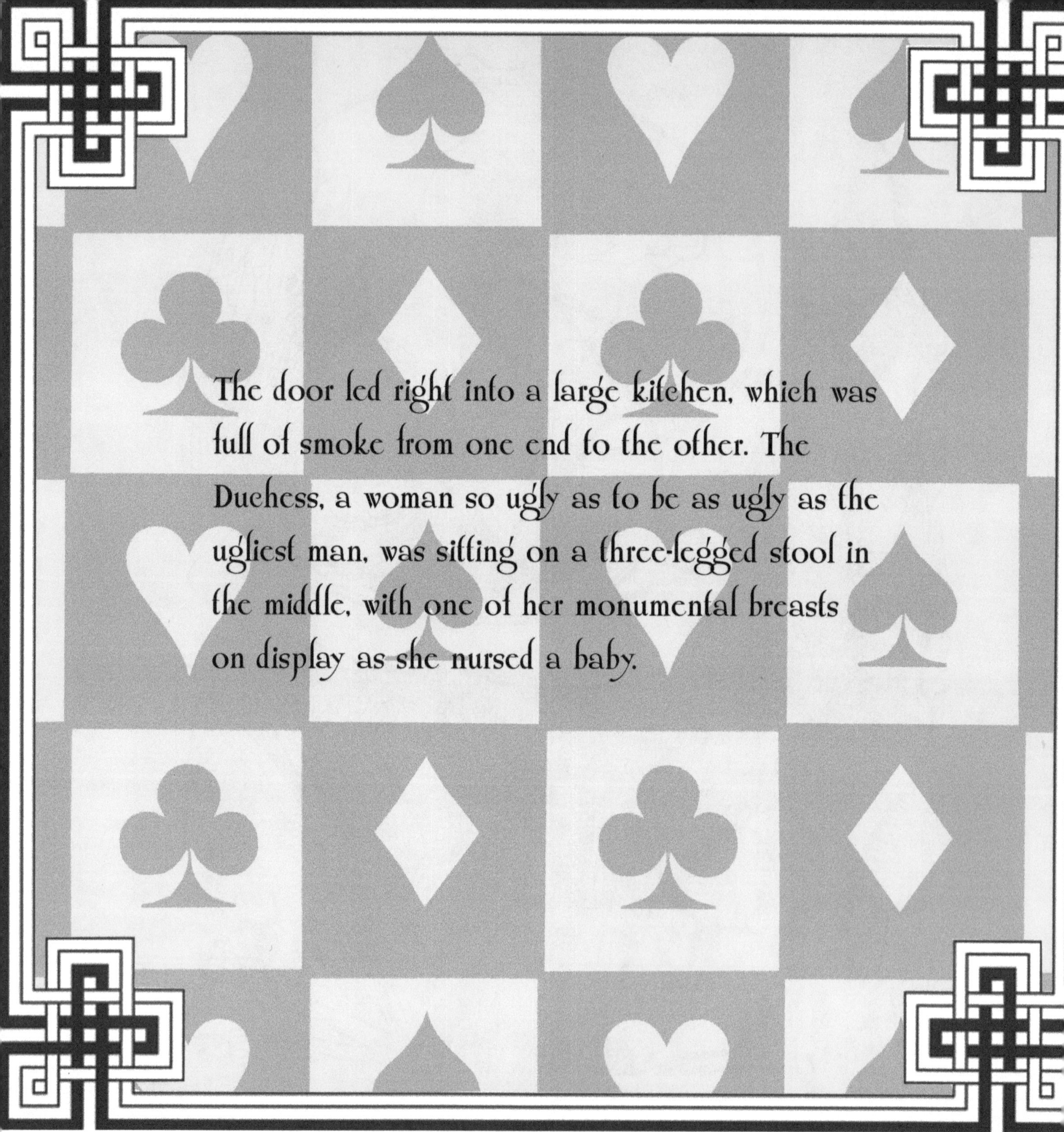

The door led right into a large kitchen, which was full of smoke from one end to the other. The Duchess, a woman so ugly as to be as ugly as the ugliest man, was sitting on a three-legged stool in the middle, with one of her monumental breasts on display as she nursed a baby.

The cat only grinned when he saw Alice. He looked good natured, she thought; still he had very long claws and a great many teeth, like a fur covered little shark, so she felt that he ought to be treated with respect. "Here, kitty, kitty" she began, rather timidly, as she did not at all know whether he would like the name. However, he only grinned a little wider. "He is so damn cute. I just want to squeeze the poop out of him," thought Alice.

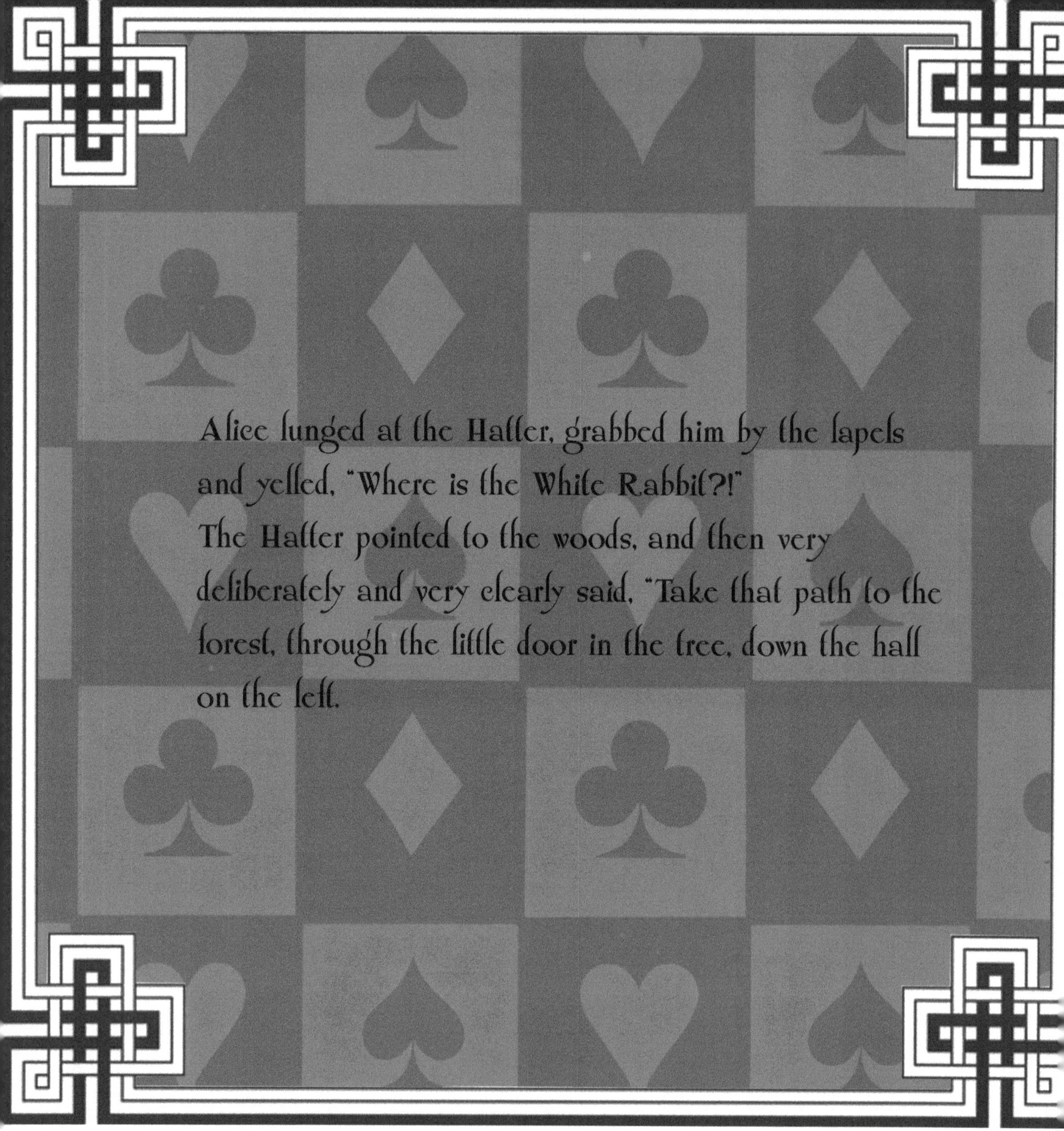

Alice lunged at the Hatter, grabbed him by the lapels and yelled, "Where is the White Rabbit?!"

The Hatter pointed to the woods, and then very deliberately and very clearly said, "Take that path to the forest, through the little door in the tree, down the hall on the left.

In this Style 10/6

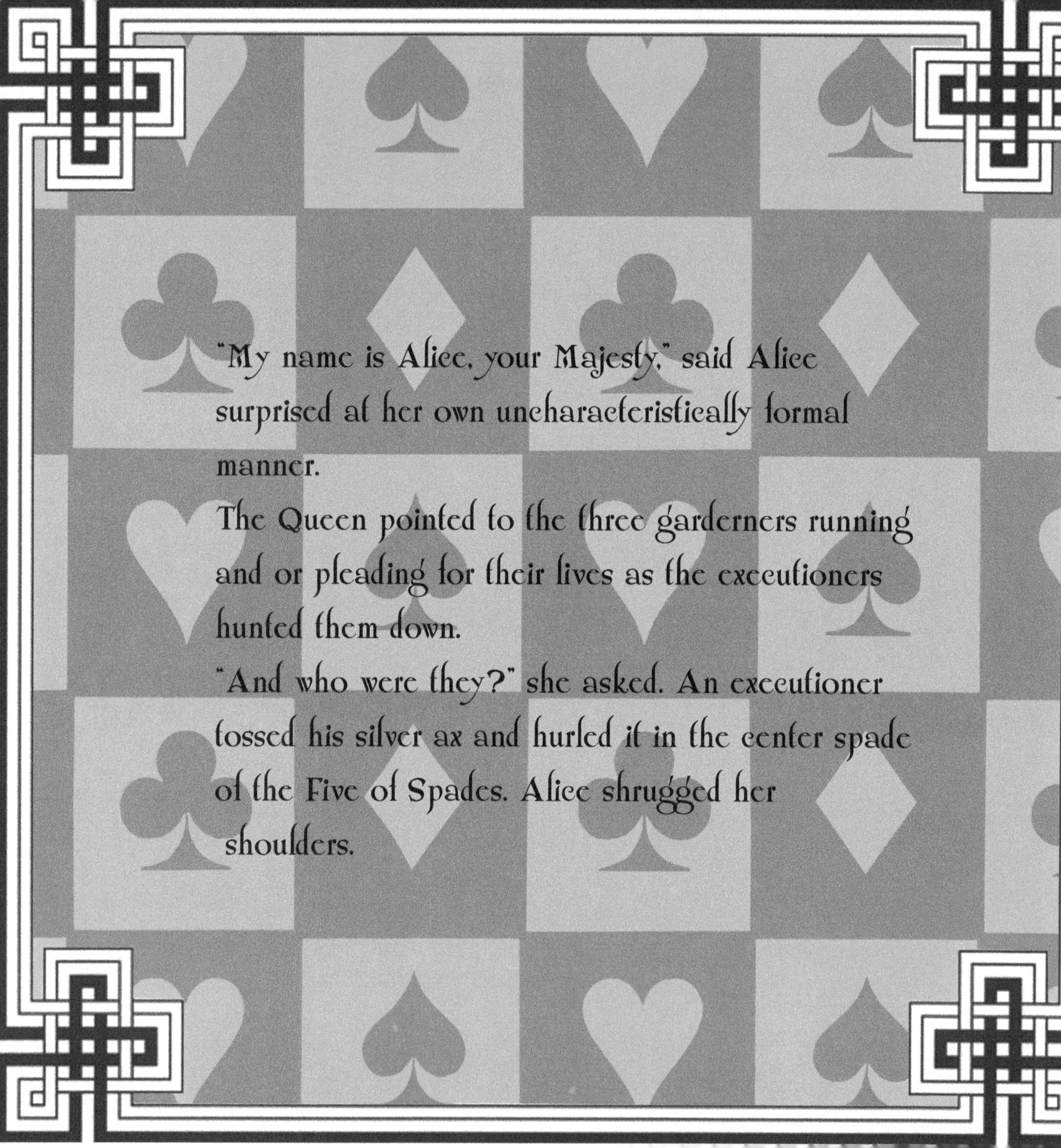

"My name is Alice, your Majesty," said Alice surprised at her own uncharacteristically formal manner.

The Queen pointed to the three garderners running and or pleading for their lives as the executioners hunted them down.

"And who were they?" she asked. An executioner tossed his silver ax and hurled it in the center spade of the Five of Spades. Alice shrugged her shoulders.

Alice couldn't believe it. "What did I tell you?" Alice pulled out her .45 and stuck it in the flamingo's face. Instantly the bird went rigid."

Alice tumbled out of the looking-glass and with a monumental thud landed upon her derriere once again; slowly and painfully she pulled herself up off of the mist covered ground, muttering, "that bitch." She leaned down, picked up her top hat, brushed it off and looked around for the first time. Alice was surprised to see she was still in the Royal maze.

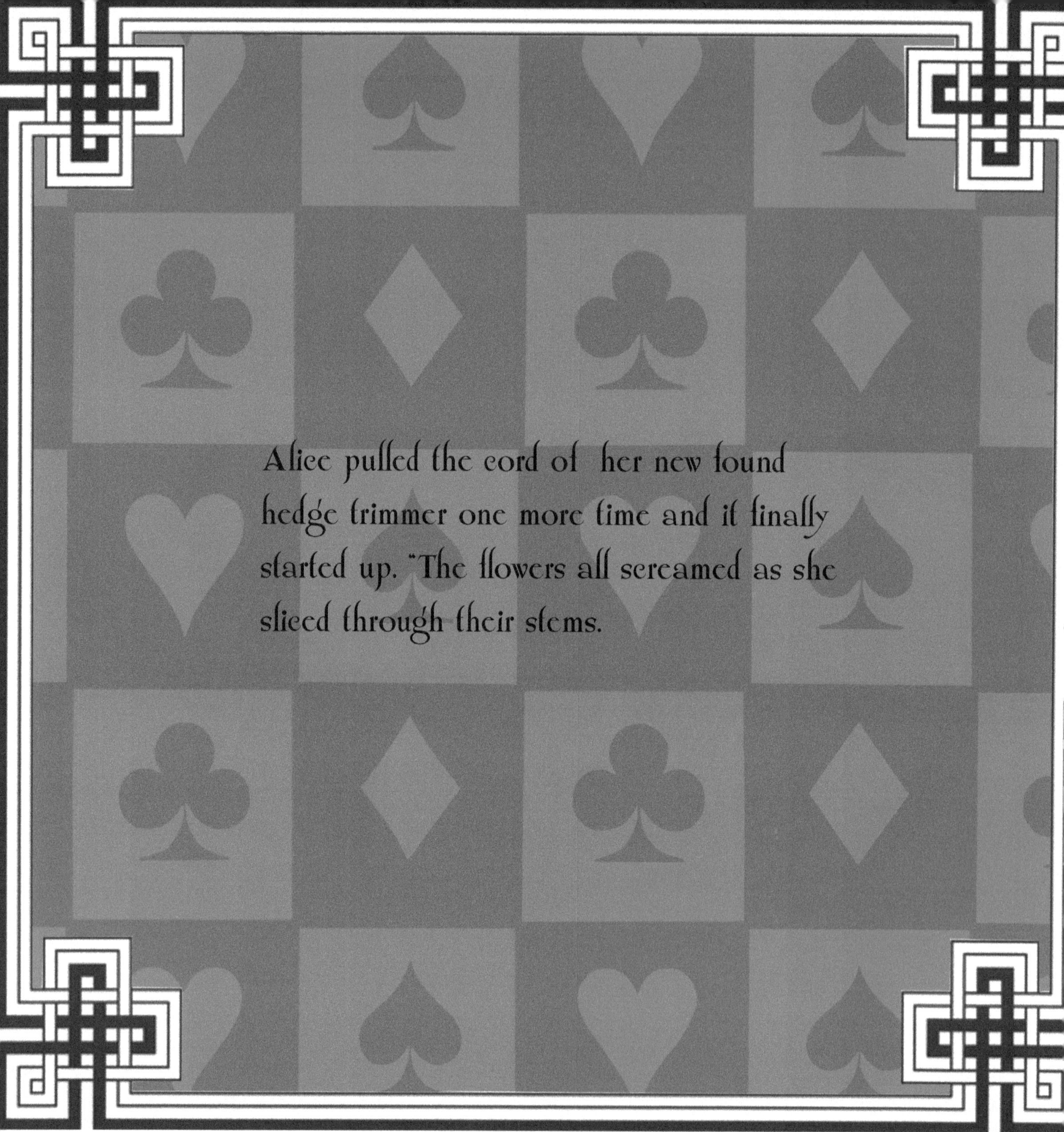

Alice pulled the cord of her new found hedge trimmer one more time and it finally started up. "The flowers all screamed as she sliced through their stems.

"I need weapons and she says you are the right guys, right?" Alice pulled out the little purse the Queen had given her and gave it a jingle, but the little men only continued to look at each other and Grin.

DEE

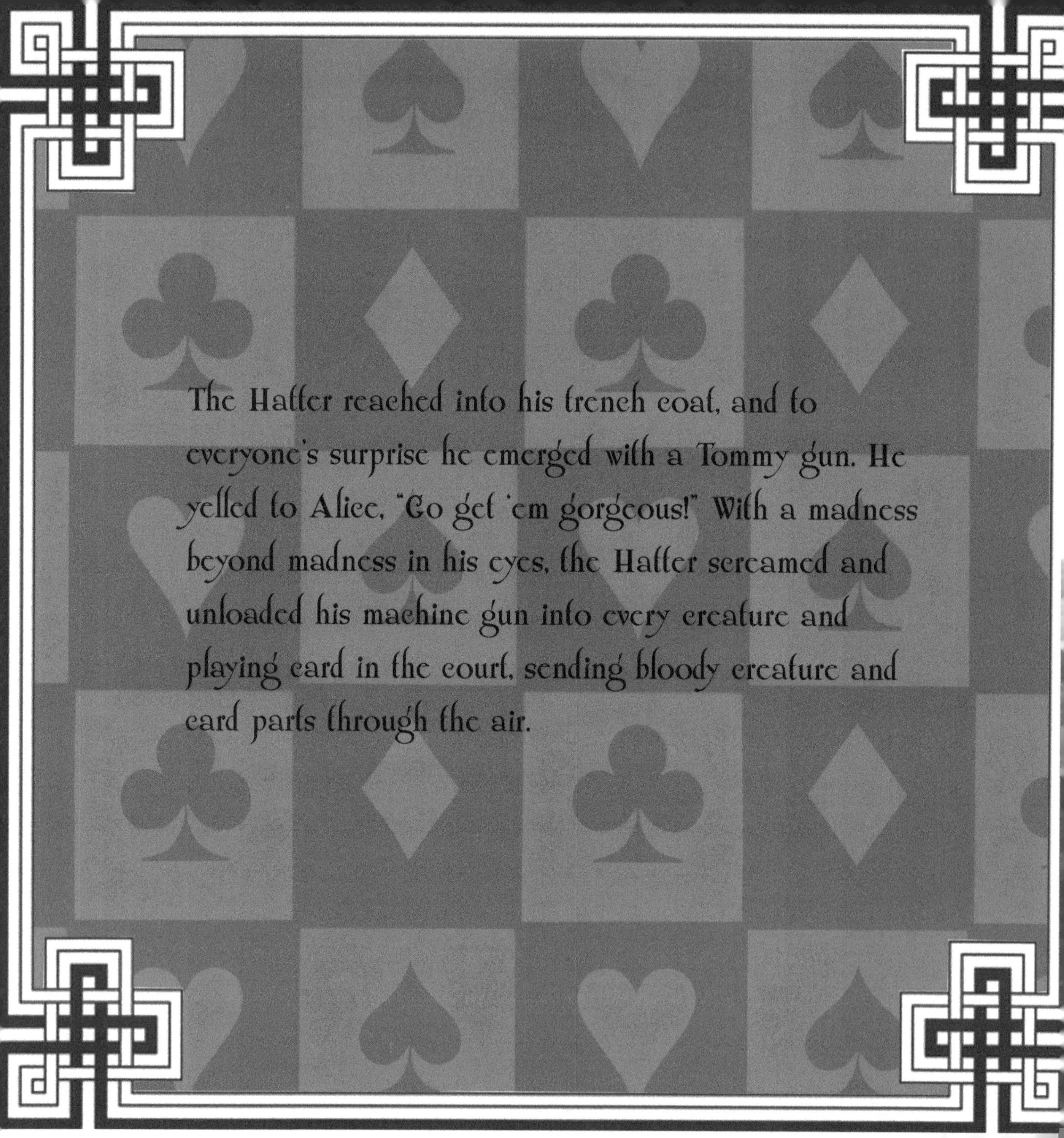

The Hatter reached into his trench coat, and to everyone's surprise he emerged with a Tommy gun. He yelled to Alice, "Go get 'em gorgeous!" With a madness beyond madness in his eyes, the Hatter screamed and unloaded his machine gun into every creature and playing card in the court, sending bloody creature and card parts through the air.

In this

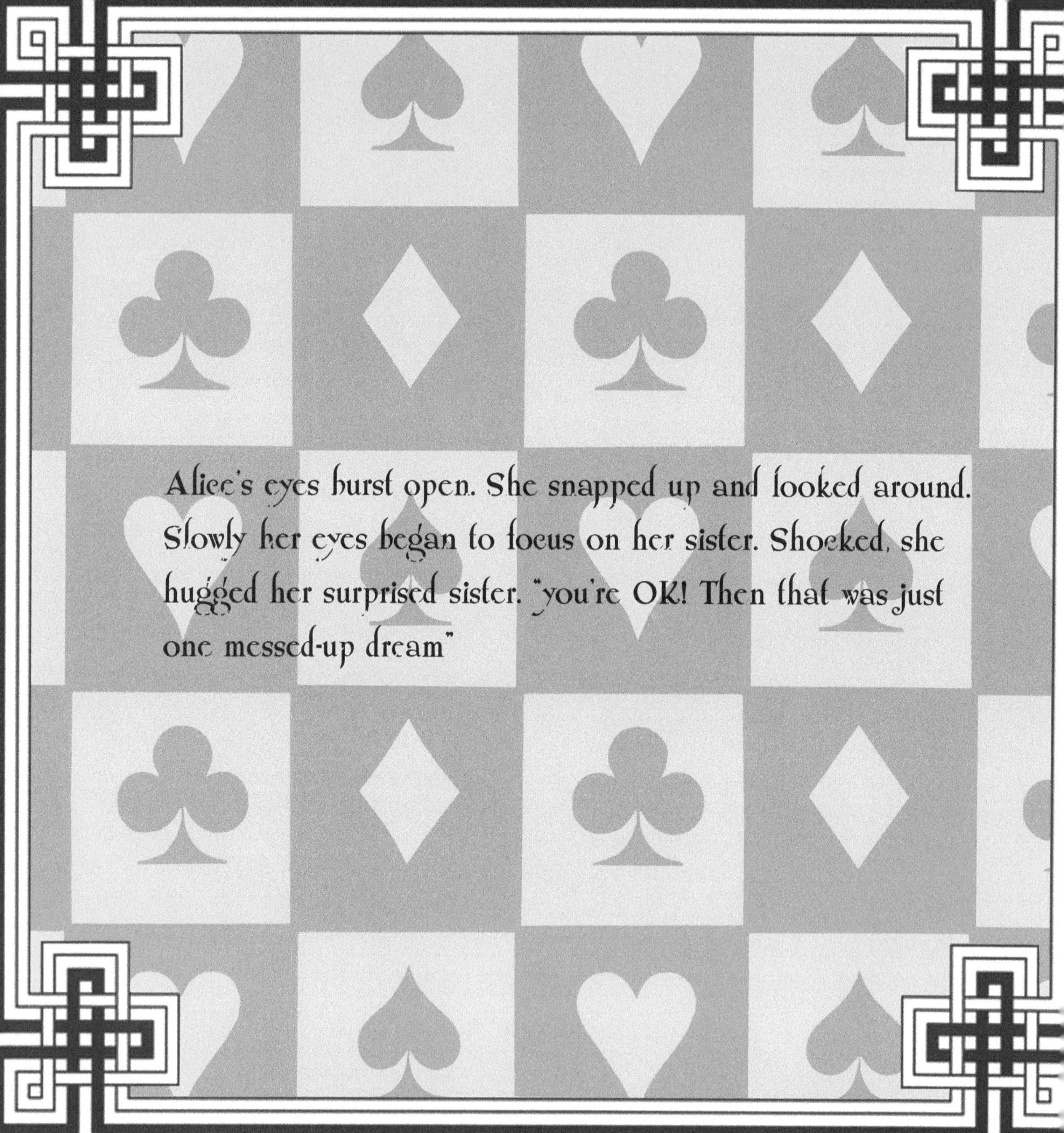

Alice's eyes burst open. She snapped up and looked around. Slowly her eyes began to focus on her sister. Shocked, she hugged her surprised sister. "you're OK! Then that was just one messed-up dream"

Author Lewis Carroll 1835-1895

Illustrator Sir John Tenniel 1820-1914

Author Raúl Alberto Contreras and his rabbit Boo Radley

www.ingramcontent.com/pod-product-compliance
Lightning Source LLC
Chambersburg PA
CBHW041640010726
47507CB00011B/414

9781936517947